LEFT: Steiff Bear, 26in (66.0cm), 1907. Value $900. **RIGHT:** Steiff Bear, 24in (61.0cm), 1905. Value $1,200. (See pages 66 & 57.)

The Teddy Bear and friends™
Price Guide

Compiled by Helen Sieverling

Edited by Albert Christian Revi

Steiff Bear on wheels, 10in (25.4cm), 1910. Value $450.
(See page 66.)

Published by  HOBBY HOUSE PRESS, INC. ™
Cumberland, Maryland 21502

DEDICATION

This book is affectionately dedicated to Sarah Ann Sieverling, Samuel Glenn Bowers, and to all who truly love Teddy Bears and soft toys and make them a joyful part of their lives.

IN APPRECIATION

My sincere thanks to all of you who gave me a helping hand in making this book possible. An Arctophile (lovers of the bear) is always happy to share their treasures and their knowledge as well as their time. I am especially indebted to Mr. Ken Bird, Elke Block, Sally Bowen, Samuel Glenn Bowers, Bob and Rebecca Collins, the Collins Family, Denise Grey, Sheri Stotz-Hanson of the *Boutonniere Newsletter*, Margaret Mandel, Mabel May, Martha McCarter, Ruth Morris, Ethel Pistole, Raymond and Robin Sieverling, Sarah Ann Sieverling, Steven Sieverling, Grace Steuri, Billie Tyrrell, Judy Johnson and Joyce Colvig. Thanks to John Schoonmaker and Glenn Sieverling for the lovely photographs.

A special thank you to Pat Schoonmaker for her support and knowledgeable help, and last but not least, I would like to say a very Special Thank You to Mr. Gary R. Ruddell and Mr. A. Christian Revi, both of HOBBY HOUSE PRESS for making it all happen.

Oh yes, many thanks to Susan Bowers, my secretary, who always knew what I meant even when I said it wrong. She made the letters sound wonderful.

LEFT TO RIGHT: Steiff Rabbit, 11in (27.9cm), c.1950. Value $75. Schuco Bear, 40in (91.6cm), c.1939. Value $600. Steiff "Waldi" Dog, 9in (22.9cm), 1957. Value $100. (See pages 134, 48 & 108.)

Steiff Tiger, 12in (19.1cm), c.1970. Value $200. (See page 148.)

FOREWORD

Teddy Bear collectors are a group set apart from collectors of anything I have ever known. Once you love a Teddy Bear it is as though it comes alive and you never need to be lonely again. People who collect Teddy Bears are generally loving and caring people. A tiny baby will respond with a smile when one is held up for it to see. An elderly person in a convalescent home, when given one, will hug it to himself and he has an instant friend and feels loved. Teddy Bears are just pure happiness. There is an army of collectors of *TEDDY BEAR AND FRIENDS* that is growing everyday. This Price Guide is designed to be a help to them. It will be a help in evaluating a bear or soft toy. Please keep in mind two bears alike, made in a given year are not necessarily of the same value. One may be mint and the other may be almost beyond restoration. Allowances must be made.

The Teddy Bear, as such, is approximately eighty years of age and while some have survived beautifully, others have met with natural enemies and neglect.

I am not claiming to be 100% accurate, but to the best of my ability, am giving a true evaluation. I have noted the prices of items for sale at Teddy Bear functions, Doll Shows and Auctions, and have taken an "average" to arrive at the values given.

Fortunately, I have had access to wonderful sources of information including Pat Schoonmaker's book, *A Collector's History of the Teddy Bear*, and a dozen toy catalogues of bygone years which were used for checking the age of an animal when buttons and tags were missing, many Teddy Bear publications from clubs, and information from overseas.

There have been many wonderful houses both here and abroad who have designed and made bears and soft toys for us to enjoy. I would like to mention a few whose products are evaluated in this book.

MERRYTHOUGHT
England

Oliver Homes is the Director of the company. He was a guest speaker at the Teddy Bear Booster Club in California this year. He told us the word "Merrythought" means a forked bone of a bird or even the largest part of that bone broken between two companions. The Merrythought "Wishbone Shape" is the company's trademark. This company has always been a family owned business. They started out as a mohair weaving business and in 1930 formed the Merrythought Soft Toy Company. They attended their first Toy Fair in 1931.

IDEAL

The Ideal Toy Company made their first Teddy Bear shortly after the Teddy Roosevelt refusal to shoot the bear and the cartoon appeared in the paper in 1902.

Morris Michtom was the founder of the Ideal Toy Corporation of America. Mr. Michtom is accredited with giving Teddy Bears their name.

The Company is still in business today and have given much to the toy world including the ever popular Shirley Temple Doll as well as the "Ideal" Teddy Bear.

HOUSE OF NISBET

In 1953, Peggy Nisbet made her first doll. Her doll making has been so successful it has opened up new avenues, one of which is soft toy making.

The House of Nisbet is located in England, Dunster Park, Winscombe, and they have just recently moved to their new premises.

Bully Bear was inspired by Peter Bull, a Hobby House "Regular" and was created by Peggy Nesbit. Other Nesbit bears have been Scottish Bear, the Cowboy and the Quinn's Jubilee Bear.

KNICKERBOCKER TOY COMPANY

There is very little information on this company. I do know they have produced many "Disney" toys.

BRUIN MANUFACTURING COMPANY
1907

This company's trademark was a label in gold letters on each piece usually on the foot stamped with the trademark, "B.M.C."

STEIFF

"Only the best is good enough for our Children" was the motto Margarete Steiff started this company with. These Bears and soft toys have an irresistible appeal with their longer arms, ever so slightly turned up noses, large humps and big feet. There is nothing I can imagine that would cause a true collector's blood to race in his veins more than the thought that he just might acquire another early Steiff Bear.

Margarete Steiff first opened her shop in 1880. Great care and precision sewing has always been a part of Steiff. One of the present day slogans of this very successful company is, "A Steiff is Forever Yours."

It might be of help to you, as it was for me, upon finding the age of the bear or animal if a Steiff Button is still intact.

STEIFF BUTTONS

Printed "Steiff" Prewar 1945
U.S. Zone (might be a cloth tag 1948-1949)

Raised Script 1950-1960.

Indented Script 1960-1981.

Gold Button 1982.

In 1958 on the 100th Anniversary of Teddy Roosevelt's birth, the Hamlet of Giengen, (Steiff's Home) organized a Teddy Bear Festival and over 25,000 people from all over Europe attended. The Steiff Company is presently still engaged in making Teddies and their friends.

GEBRUDER SUSSENGUTH FACTORY
Neustadt near Coburg Thuringia

The "Peter" bears were manufactured in this factory between 1925 and 1928. A hundred of these bears were found in a warehouse in Germany. These "Peter" bears were quite ferocious looking and were unsold when a toy shop closed down. Of course, this factory is no longer in business.

Steiff Horses and Carriage. Horses, 27in (68.6cm), c.1910. Value $600 each. Carriage, 51in (125.9cm), c.1910. Value $1,000. (See pages 97 & 120).

Steiff "Zotty," 33in (83.8cm), c.1970. Value $600. (See page 86.)

CHAD VALLEY

This house opened in England in 1897, but did not register the name "Chad Valley" until 1920.

These bears are usually identified by a cloth tag sewn on the foot which reads:

"BY APPOINTMENT TOY
MAKERS TO H.M.
QUEEN ELIZABETH
THE QUEEN MOTHER"

HERMANN

Hermann is a company in Germany who has imported heavily to the United States for the last several years. Aside from their wonderful Teddy Bears, they make cats, monkeys, and other soft animal toys. They also make many limited editions.

(*) Items that have been illustrated in Patricia N. Schoonmaker's book, *A Collector's History of the Teddy Bear*, have been noted thus:
CHTB ill. (number)

CAN'T FIND YOUR BEAR?

If you are unable to locate your Teddy Bear or other animal toy in this price guide, just send us a good quality photo of your toy and a full description of it patterned after those listed in this guide, and the author will reply personally giving you whatever information she can. Send your questions to Mrs. Helen Sieverling, C/o Hobby House Press, Inc., 900 Frederick Street, Cumberland, Maryland 21502. (A self-addressed and stamped envelope is requested.)

LEFT: Geb. Sussenguth "Peter" Bear, silver-gray, 14in (35.6cm), c.1925. Value $900. **RIGHT:** Geb. Sussenguth "Peter" Bear, dark brown, 14in (35.6cm), c.1925. Value $800. (See page 22.)

LEFT: Steiff Cock, 11in (27.9cm), 1960. Value $150. **RIGHT:** Steiff Hen, 9in (22.9cm), 1960. Value $150. (See pages 103 & 120.)

This book belongs to

_____

_____

_____

TABLE OF CONTENTS

Dedication 3

In Appreciation 3

Foreword (including history of
   manufacturers) 6

Can't Find Your Bear? 11

Aetna 17

American Character 17

Averill 17

Bluine Manufacturing Co. 18

Bruin Manufacturing Co. 18

Chad Valley 18

Charm Co. Korea 20

Columbia T B Mfg. Co. 20

Dakin 21

Deetz 21

G. C. Gillespie 22

Gebruder Sussenguth 22

Gund 23

Hermann 22/24

Ideal 25

Kersa 32

Knickerbocker 33

M. C. Z. (Switzerland) 36

Merry Thought 36

Madame Alexander 37

Nisbet 39

Petz 39

R. D. France 40

Rose Mary Originals 42

Rushton Co 43

Schuco 43

Shackman 50

Steiff 51

Strauss 150

Unknown Manufacturers 151

Wilkinson Mfg. Co. 210

Related Items 212

Aetna   14in(35.6cm) Bear(*)   c1906
    Gold mohair; shoe button eyes; jtd. legs
    & arms; swivel head; straw stuffing.
    (*)Stamped "Aetna" on foot.
    Aetna on foot. Mint condition. $250

Aetna   12in(30.5cm) Bear(*)   1907
    Alternated pink & blue plush; shoe button
    eyes; jtd. legs & arms; sw. head; straw
    stuffing. (*)Clown; CHTB ill. 49.
    Aetna on foot. Worn condition. $275

American Char. 12in(30.5cm) Bear(*)   c1970
    Tan plush; glass eyes; jtd. legs & arms;
    swivel head; cotton stuffing. (*)Vinyl
    face.
    No ID mark.   Good condition. $65

ABOVE LEFT:
Averill(German) 5in(12.0cm) Cat   c1930
    All=bisque gray body w/ green eyes; jtd.
    legs & arms; marked on back "Cop.R by
    Georgene Averill/890/Germany."
    Incised & tag. Mint condition. $1,200
ABOVE RIGHT:
Averill   5in(12.0cm) Dog(*)   c1930
    (*)"Rag"; all-bisque wht. body w/ black
    spots; blue braided yarn tail; brn glass
    eyes; incised on back "Rag"/Geo. Averill.
    Incised marks. Mint condition. $1,200

Bluine Mfg.   10in(25.4cm) Bear(*)   1915
    Gold plush; shoe but. eyes; jtd. legs &
    arms; sw. head; straw stuff; (*)Premium
    for selling Bluine. CHTB Ill. 162.
    No ID mark.   Worn condition. $75

ABOVE:
Bruin Mfg. Co.   13in(33.0cm) Bear   1907
    Gold mohair; shoe button eyes; jointed
    legs & arms; swivel head; straw stuffing.
    Label,foot,BMC. Excellent cond. $500

Bruin Mfg. Co.   12in(30.5cm) Bear   1926
    Tan mohair; shoe button eyes; jointed
    legs & arms; swivel head; straw stuffing.
    No ID mark.   Slightly worn. $300

Chad Valley   19in(45.7cm) Bear   c1930
    Gold mohair; shoe button eyes; jointed
    legs & arms; swivel head; straw stuffing.
    No ID mark.   Mint condition. $195

Chad Valley   14in(35.6cm) Bear   c1940
    Dk. brown mohair; glass eyes; jtd. legs,
    arms&head; kapok stuffing; By Appointment
    Toy Maker to H.M. Queen Elizabeth, Qu.Mo.
    Tag on foot.   Worn condition. $195

Chad Valley   13in(33.0cm) Bear   c1950
    Blue mohair; glass eyes; jointed legs &
    arms; swivel head; straw stuffing.
    No ID mark.   Good condition. $195

ABOVE:
Chad Valley   12in(30.5cm) Cat(*)   c1940
    (*)"Felix the Cat"; blk. mohair w/black
    felt ears; long tail; gl. eyes; jtd. legs
    & arms; sw. head; straw stuffing.
    No ID mark.   Excellent cond. $275

19

BELOW LEFT:
Charm Co. Korea 13in(31.8cm) Bear(*)   c1980
    Tan syn. plush; plastic eyes; jtd. legs &
    arms; sw. head; cot. stuffing; (*)blue
    T-shirt w/ "Teddy Booster" on front.
    Cloth tag.   Excellent cond. $15

ABOVE RIGHT:
Columbia T B Mf 17in(43.2cm) Bear(*)   1907
    "Laughing Roosevelt"; red-rust mohair;
    shoe button eyes; jtd.legs & arms; swivel
    head; (*)mou. opens,shows gl & ptd teeth.
    No ID mark.   Excellent cond. $500

Dakin   8in(20.3cm) Bear(*)   1979
  (*) "Misha"; lt. brown plush w/ felt
  claws plastic eyes & nose; not jointed;
  Olympic emblem on belt.
  Emblem on belt. Mint condition. $8

Dakin   18in(45.7cm) Bear(*)   1979
  (*)"Misha"; lt. brn. plush w/ white nose
  & front; black felt claws; Olympic emblem
  on belt; made for 1980 Winter Olympics.
  Emblem on belt. Mint condition. $35

Dakin   22in(55.9cm) Bear(*)   1979
  (*)"Misha";lt. brn. plush w/ felt claws;
  plastic eyes & nose;not jointed; olympic
  emblem belt; made for 1980 Winter Olymp.
  Tags.   Mint condition. $45

Dakin   21in(53.3cm) Bear(*)   1980
  (*)"Misha Olympic Bear." Dk. brown plush;
  felt eyes; not jointed; kapok stuffing.
  Label & tag.   Mint condition. $45
BELOW:
Deetz   16in(40.6cm) Bear(*)   1977
  Deetz Crocker Bank Advertising; tan
  plush; plastic eyes; not jointed; kapok
  stuffing.
  Tag & label.   Mint condition. $12

G.C. Gillespie   16in(40.6cm) Bear(*)   1907
    Lt. brn. plush over metal body; shoe but.
    eyes; jtd. legs & arms; sw. head; (*)Tum-
    bling Cub; mech. not working; CHTB il.191
    No ID mark.   Worn condition. $100

Geb. Sussenguth 14in(35.6cm) Bear(*)   c1925
    (*)"Peter"; dk. brown mohair; brn. felt
    pads; wooden eyes; jtd. legs & arms; open
    mouth w/teeth; tongue moves; sw. head.
    Paper tag.   Mint-in-box. $800

Geb. Sussenguth 14in(35.6cm) Bear(*)   c1925
    (*)"Peter"; silver-gray mohair; peach
    felt pads; gl. googly moving eyes; joint-
    ed legs & arms; sw. head; straw stuffing.
    Paper tag.   Mint-in-box. $900

Grisley Marke   15in(38.1cm) Bear(*)   c1949
    Dark brown; synthetic fabric; glass eyes;
    jtd. legs & arms; sw. head; kapok stuff;
    (*)metal button on chest "Grisley Marke."
    Metal button.   Excellent cond. $100
BELOW:
Hermann   16in(40.6cm) Bear(*)   c1930
    Very lt. brown plush; glass eyes; jointed
    legs & arms; swivel head; straw stuffing
    (*)talking, pull tape in his back.
    No ID mark.   Mint condition. $250

ABOVE:
Gund   28in(71.1cm) Wolf(*)   c1960
    (*)"Willie the Wolf." Blk. mohair; paint-
    ed eyes; not jtd; kapok stuff; wears chk.
    pants & red felt coat; orig. knife/chain.
    Cloth tag.   Good to excel. $150

ABOVE:
Hermann   11in(27.9cm) Donkey(*) c1950
   Gray mohair; wht. inner ears; glass eyes;
   not jointed; straw stuffing; original
   saddle; (*) on wheels.
   Tag.   Mint cond. $100

BELOW:
Hermann   20in(50.8cm) Bear   c1950
   Tan mohair; glass eyes; jtd. legs & arms;
   swivel head; straw stuffing.
   No ID mark.   Slightly worn. $235

ABOVE:

Hermann 24in (61.0cm) Bear c1900
Gold mohair; shoe button eyes; jointed
legs & arms; swivel head; straw stuffing.
No ID mark. Replaced pads. $350

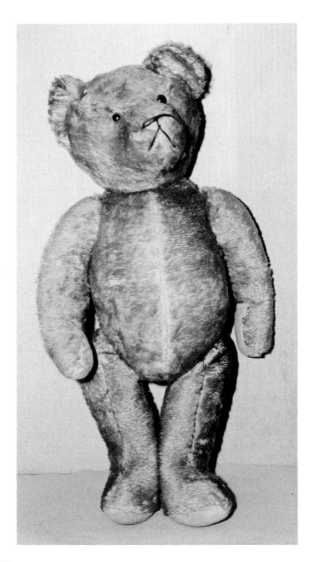

ABOVE:
Ideal   23in(58.4cm) Bear   1910
    Gold mohair; glas eyes; jtd. legs & arms;
    swivel head; straw stuffing; chubby w/
    nice hump on back.
    No ID mark.   Excellent cond. $500

Ideal   24in(61.0cm) Bear   1910
    Gold mohair; shoe button eyes; jtd. arms/
    legs; swivel head; straw stuffing; has
    short arms & nose.
    No ID mark.   Excellent cond. $200

BELOW:
Ideal   24in(61.0cm) Bear   1920
    Gold mohair; glass eyes; jointed legs &
    arms; swivel head; straw stuffing.
    No ID mark.   Excellent cond. $375

Ideal   16in(40.6cm) Bear   1924
   Gold mohair; shoe button eyes; long
   jointed legs & arms; swivel head; straw
   stuffing.
   No ID mark.   Worn condition. $200

Ideal   11in(27.9cm) Bear(*)   1945
   (*)"Running Brown Bear"; dk. brown soft,
   silky plush;glass eyes; not jointed; cotton stuffing; standing 9in(22.9cm) high.
   No ID mark.   Mint condition. $30

Ideal   15in(38.1cm) Bear(*)   1945
   (*)"Ideal Honey Bear"; lt. brown & ivory
   plush; glass eyes; swivel head; cotton
   stuffing.
   No ID mark.   Mint condition. $25

Ideal   21in(53.3cm) Bear   1945
   Brown plush w/white torso & pads; glass
   eyes; not jointed; cotton stuffing.
   No ID mark.   Mint condition. $35

Ideal   23in(58.4cm) Bear(*)   1945
   (*)"Billy Bear"; gold mohair; glass eyes;
   jointed legs & arms; swivel head; kapok
   stuffing.
   No ID mark.   Mint condition. $45

OPPOSITE PAGE ABOVE:
Ideal   16in(40.6cm) Bear(*)   1953
   (*)"Smokey"; first edition; cinnamon br-
   own w/blue pants & brown hat; vinyl head
   & paws; sw. head; not jtd; kapok stuffing
   Tag.   Mint condition. $125

OPPOSITE PAGE BELOW:
Ideal   20in(50.8cm) Bear(*)   1954
   (*)"Smokey"; rust plush body & feet;
   plastic head & eyes; not jointed; hat &
   shovel missing.
   Cloth tag.   Worn condition. $45

ABOVE:
Ideal   15in(38.1cm) Bear(*)   1978
  (*)Teddy Bear 75th Birthday;tan nylon bo-
  dy; plastic eyes; not jointed; nylon fi-
  bre stuffing. Stitched nose, ears, pads.
  Paper tag.   Mint-in-box. $45

ABOVE:
Ideal   12in(30.5cm) Bear(*)   1981
   (*) Good Bears of the World; tan syn. fur
   w/ painted toes & pads; plastic eyes; not
   jointed; syn. stuffing.
   Paper tag.   Mint condition. $8

Ideal   12in(30.5cm) Panda(*)   1945
   (*)"Ideal Panda - Stand Alone"; black and
   white rayon fleece; not jointed; cotton
   stuffing.
   No ID mark.   Mint condition. $25

Ideal   18in(44.5cm) Panda(*)   1945
   (*)"Peter Panda"; black & white rayon
   fleece; celluloid eyes; not jointed; kapok stuffing.
   No ID mark.   Mint condition. $25

BELOW:
Kersa   11in(27.9cm) Bear   c1930
   Gold mohair; glass eyes; jointed legs &
   arms; swivel head; straw stuffing; metal
   tag on both feet; "Kersa German."
   Metal tag.   Excellent cond. $200

ABOVE:
Knickerbocker   16in(40.6cm) Bear   c1930
   White mohair; glass eyes; jointed legs &
   arms; swivel head; straw stuffing.
   No ID mark.   Mint condition. $195

Knickerbocker   17in(43.2cm) Bear   c1930
   Rust-red long mohair; rare tin decal eyes;
   jointed legs & arms; swivel head; lt. tan
   sheared mohair nose; straw stuffing.
   No ID mark.   Pads rep. o/w gd. $200

BELOW LEFT:
Knickerbocker   26in(66.0cm) Bear   c1930
    Very lt. brown long mohair; glass eyes;
    jointed legs & arms; swivel head; straw
    stuffing.
    No ID mark.   Slightly worn. $325

BELOW RIGHT:
Knickerbocker   40in(91.6cm) Bear   c1939
    Dark brown mohair; shoe button eyes; jtd.
    legs & arms; swivel head; straw stuffing.
    No ID mark.   Excellent cond. $600

Knickerbocker   6in(15.2cm) Bear   c1940
    Gold plush; glass eyes; jointed legs &
    arms; cotton stuffing.
    No ID mark.   Mint condition. $45

Knickerbocker   13in(33.0cm) Bear   1940
    White mohair; glass eyes; jointed legs &
    arms; swivel head; kapok stuffing.
    No ID mark.   Worn condition. $150

Knickerbocker   14in(35.6cm) Bear   c1950
    White mohair; glass eyes; jointed legs &
    arms; swivel head; kapok stuffing.
    No ID mark.   Worn condition. $195
BELOW:
Knickerbocker   14in(35.6cm) Bear   c1960
    Lt. brown mohair w/white face; glass
    eyes; jointed legs & arms; swivel head;
    straw stuffing.
    No ID mark.   Excellent cond. $100

M.C.Z. (Swiss)   9in(22.9cm) Bear(*)   c1960
    (*)"Mutzli"; lt. brown mohair; felt pads
    w/stitched claws; gl. eyes; jtd. legs &
    arms; sw. head; music box; CHTB ill. 477.
    Button in ear.   Excellent cond. $200

Merry Thought   22in(55.9cm) Orang.(*) c1940
    Gold mohair; shoe but. eyes; jtd. legs &
    arms;sw. head; str.& kap. stuff. (*)two-
    faced bear & orangutan on orangutan body.
    Cloth tag.   Excellent cond. $700

LEFT TO RIGHT:

Mme. Alexander 11in(27.9cm) Pig c1940
    Composition body; painted eyes; jtd. legs
    & arms; swivel head; wearing pink shorts,
    blue jacket & white hat & shoes.
    Tag & on back. Excellent cond. $200

Mme. Alexander 11in(27.9cm) Pig c1940
    Composition body; painted eyes; jtd. legs
    & arms; swivel head;clothes not original.
    Mme. Alexander. Worn condition. $125

Mme. Alexander 11in(27.9cm) Pig c1940
    Composition body; painted eyes; jtd. legs
    & arms; wearing blue overalls, white hat
    & gloves, black & white shoes.
    Tag & on back. Excellent cond. $200

Mme. Alexander   14in(35.6cm) Rabbit(*) c1930
   (*)"Uncle Wiggly"; lt. tan cotton with
   painted face & pink inner ear; glass eyes
   & swivel head; not jtd; clothes not orig.
   No ID mark.   Good condition. $100

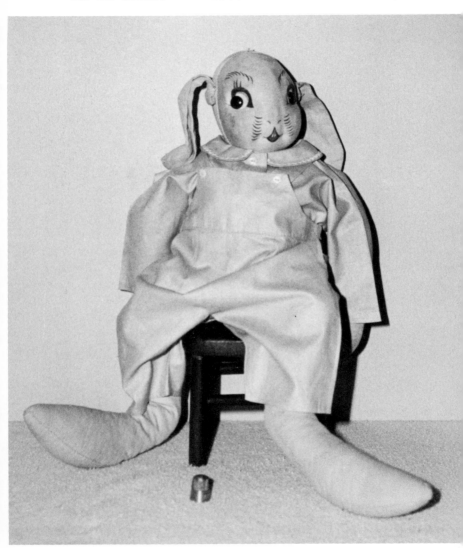

ABOVE RIGHT:
Nisbet   18in(45.7cm) Bear(*)   1980
   (*) "Bully Bear"; gold mohair; glass eyes
   jtd. legs & arms; swivel head; tag reads:
   "Bully Bear."
   Tags.   Mint-in-box. $125

ABOVE LEFT:
Steiff   17in(43.2cm) Bear(*)   1980
   (*) 100th Anniversary bear; gold mohair;
   felt pads; glass eyes; jtd. legs & arms;
   sw. head; 5,000 U.S. 6,000 Europe.
   Ltd. edition.
   Tag & button.   Mint-in-box. $350

Petz   4in(10.2cm) Bear   c1930
   Gold extra long mohair; glass eyes; jtd.
   legs & arms; straw stuffing.
   Tag on front.   Mint condition. $65

ABOVE:
R.D. France   11in(27.9cm) Bear(*)   c1895
  Dk.brown & white rabbit fur; glass stick-
  pin eyes; not jointed; (*)Mechanical key-
  wind; bear dances on metal-sole feet.
  R.D. on key.   Mint condition. $1,000

R.D. France   15in(38.1cm) Bear(*)   c1930
  Dk. brown fur; shoe button eyes; jointed
  forearms; swivel head; straw & mechanism
  stuffing; (*)stands; plays cymbals.
  No ID mark.   Needs repairs. $550

BELOW:
R.D. France   15in(38.1cm) Koala(*)   c1930
   Dk. brown & white rabbit fur; glass eyes;
   not jointed; (*) mechanical, pours liquid
   fr. pewter btl. into jigger; recycles.
   No ID mark.   Mint condition. $1,200

ABOVE LEFT:
R.D.Co.(France) 12in(30.5cm) Rabbit(*) c1900
    White rabbit fur; glass eyes; not join-
    ted; fur over papier mache frame. (*)key
    wind-up clockworks toy; rabbit knits.
    R.D. on key.   Excellent cond. $1,200

ABOVE RIGHT:
Rose Mary Orig. 16in(40.6cm) Bear(*)   1953
    (*)"Travel Sleepy Bear" Travel-Lodge Adv.
    cinnamon plush; felt eyes; not jointed;
    Copyrt. C. Beaver; white shirt.
    Button.   Mint condition. $15

ABOVE:

Rushton Co.   12in(30.5cm) Bear(*)   c1977
 White synthetic fabric w/red inner ear,
 red felt tongue & black felt nose; plastic blue eyes; tag reads (*) "Love Me."
 Paper tag.   Mint condition. $25

Schuco   11in(27.9cm) Bear   1923
 Gold mohair head & feet; sewn on clothes
 of felt; glass stickpin eyes; "yes-no
 Bell Hop Bear." jtd. legs/arms;sw. head.
 No ID mark.   Mint condition. $400

43

Schuco   11in(27.9cm) Bear(*) 1926
  Gold mohair; glass eyes; jtd. legs &
  arms; swivel head; straw stuff.; (*)moves
  head "yes" & "no" by moving tail.
  No ID mark. Mint condition. $250

ABOVE:
Schuco   17in(43.2cm) Bear(*)   1926
   Tan mohair; glass eyes; jtd. legs & arms;
   swivel head; (*)shakes head "yes" or "no"
   when tail is moved.
   No ID mark.   Excellent cond. $500

Schuco   4in(10.2cm) Bear(*)   c1930
   Dk. brown mohair; glass stickpin eyes;
   jointed legs & arms; swivel head; (*)fab-
   ric-covered metal body.
   No ID mark.   Mint condition. $75

Schuco   4in(10.2cm) Bear   c1930
   Black & white lower torso, white head;
   black ears; glass stickpin eyes; jointed
   legs & arms; sw. head; metal frame body.
   No ID mark.   Mint condition. $75

Schuco   4in(10.2cm) Bear   c1930
   Green mohair over metal frame body; glass
   stickpin eyes; jointed legs & arms; swivel head.
   No ID mark.   Mint condition. $75

Schuco   4in(10.2cm) Bear   c1930
   Gold mohair over metal frame body; glass
   stickpin eyes; jointed legs & arms.
   No ID mark.   Mint condition. $75

OPPOSITE PAGE, ABOVE:
Schuco   5in(12.7cm) Bear(*)   c1930
   Gold mohair; glass stickpin eyes; jointed
   legs & arms; (*)mechanical "Yes-No" Bear.
   No ID mark.   Excellent cond. $150

OPPOSITE PAGE, BELOW:
Schuco   5in(12.0cm) Bear(*)   c1930
   Gold mohair on metal frame; gl. stickpin
   eyes; jointed legs & arms; swivel head;
   (*)perfume bottle.
   No ID mark.   Mint condition. $200

47

ABOVE:
Schuco   17in(43.2cm) Bear(*)   c1930
   Curly white mohair; glass eyes; jtd. legs
   & arms; swivel head; straw stuffing;looks
   like yes/no bear, (*) not mechanical.
   No ID mark.   Good condition. $300

Schuco   9in(22.9cm) Bear(*)   c1949
   (*)"Tricky"; tan mohair head, paws &
   feet; gl. eyes; jtd. legs & arms; swivel
   head; straw stuff; humanized body clothed
   Plastic tag.   Mint condition. $100

Schuco   4in(8.9cm) Bear(*)   c1950
   Gold plush; glass stickpin eyes; jointed
   legs & arms; swivel head; (*)covered metal body; two-faced regular & tongue out.
   No ID mark.   Mint condition. $195

BELOW:
Schuco (?)   9in(22.9cm) Chimp(*) c1930
    White mohair; brown glass eyes; jtd. legs
    & arms; removable head; papier mache
    frame; (*)bottle.
    No ID mark.   Excellent cond. $300

ABOVE:
Schuco(?)   5in(12.7cm) Monkey(*) c1930
   Red mohair; painted metal eyes;jointed
   legs & arms; papier mache frame; (*)tumb-
   ler.
No ID mark.   Excellent cond. $85

Shackman   3in(6.4cm) Bear   c1930
   Tan plush; glass stickpin eyes; jointed
   legs & arms; swivel head; kapok stuffing.
No ID mark.   Mint condition. $20

ABOVE:
Steiff   12in(30.5cm) Alli.(*)   1957
   (*)"Gaty"; gold mohair w/green felt
   scales; tan felt claws; red felt open
   mouth; glass eyes; not jtd; straw stuff.
   Paper tag.   Excellent cond. $50

BELOW LEFT:
Steiff   4in(10.2cm) Bear   1905
   White mohair; glass stickpin eyes; joint-
   ed legs & arms; swivel head; straw stuff-
   ing.
   No ID mark.   Good condition. $200
BELOW RIGHT:
Steiff   4in(10.2cm) Bear   1905
   Gold mohair; glass stickpin eyes; jointed
   legs & arms; straw stuffing.
   Button in ear.   Good condition. $225

ABOVE:
Steiff   9in(22.9cm) Bear   1905
    Tan mohair; shoe button eyes; jtd. legs &
    arms; swivel head; straw stuffing.
    No ID mark.   Excellent cond. $500

BELOW:
Steiff   15in(38.1cm) Bear   1905
    White mohair; shoe button eyes; jointed
    legs & arms; swivel head; straw stuffing.
    Button in ear.   Mint condition. $600

BACK ROW LEFT:
```
Steiff           12in(30.5cm) Bear        1905
   Tan mohair; shoe button eyes; jtd. legs &
   arms; swivel head; straw stuffing.
   Button.         Excellent cond.        $550
```
BACK ROW RIGHT:
```
Steiff           15in(38.1cm) Bear        1905
   Gold mohair; shoe button eyes; jointed
   legs & arms; swivel head; straw stuffing.
   No ID mark.     Worn condition.        $500
```
FRONT ROW LEFT:
```
Steiff           12in(30.5cm) Bear        1903
   Tan mohair; shoe button eyes; jtd. legs &
   arms; swivel head. straw stuffing.
   Plain button.   40% fur missing.       $350
```
FRONT ROW RIGHT:
```
Steiff           14in(35.6cm) Bear        1905
   Gold mohair; glass eyes; jointed legs &
   arms; swivel head; straw stuffing.
   No ID mark.     Excellent cond.        $550
```

ABOVE LEFT:
Steiff   15in(38.1cm) Bear   1905
    Tan mohair; shoe button eyes; jointed
    arms & legs; swivel head; straw stuffing.
    Button in ear.   Excellent cond. $600
ABOVE RIGHT:
Steiff   16in(40.6cm) Bear   1905
    Tan mohair; shoe button eyes; jointed
    arms & legs; swivel head.
    Button in ear.   Worn, repaired. $575

ABOVE:

Steiff   16in(40.6cm) Bear   1905
   Gold mohair; shoe button eyes; jointed
   arms & legs; swivel head; straw stuffing.
   Plain button.   Excellent cond. $600

Steiff   17in(43.2cm) Bear   1905
   White mohair w/ off-white felt pads, brn.
   stitched nose; shoe button eyes; jtd.legs
   & arms; sw. head w/ center seam.
   Plain button.   Mint condition. $1,000

Steiff   19in(48.3cm) Bear(*)   1905
   White mohair; shoe button eyes; swivel
   head; (*)mounted on iron wheels; 14in
   (35.6cm) long.
   Button in ear. Excellent cond. $1,000

Steiff   20in(50.8cm) Bear   1905
   White mohair; shoe button eyes; jointed
   legs & arms; swivel head; straw stuffing.
   Button in ear. Mint condition. $900

Steiff   24in(61.0cm) Bear   c1905
   White mohair; shoe button eyes; jointed
   legs & arms; swivel head; straw stuffing.
   Button in ear. Mint condition. $1,200

Steiff   5in(12.7cm) Bear   1907
    White mohair; glass stickpin eyes; joint-
    ed legs & arms; swivel head; straw stuff-
    ing.
    Button in ear. Excellent cond. $300

Steiff   7in(19.1cm) Bear   1907
    White mohair; shoe button eyes; jointed
    legs & arms; swivel head; straw stuffing.
    Button in ear. Excellent cond. $350

Steiff   6in(15.2cm) Bear   1908
    White mohair; glass eyes; jointed legs &
    arms; swivel head; straw stuffing.
    Button in ear. Excellent cond. $300

ABOVE RIGHT:
Steiff   6in(15.2cm) Bear   1907
    White mohair; glass eyes; jointed legs &
    arms; straw stuffing.
    Button in ear. Excellent cond. $300
ABOVE LEFT:
Steiff   8in(20.3cm) Bear   1907
    Gold mohair; shoe button eyes; jointed
    legs & arms; swivel head; straw stuffing.
    Button in ear. Mint condition. $450

Steiff   5in(12.7cm) Bear(*)   c1907
    White mohair; glass eyes; jointed legs &
    arms; swivel head; straw stuffing;(*)bell
    inside makes rattle for baby. Rare.
    Cl. Tag & But. Excellent cond. $400

ABOVE:
Steiff   10in(25.4cm) Bear   1907
    Tan mohair; shoe button eyes; jointed
    legs & arms; swivel head; straw stuffing.
    No ID mark.   Mint condition. $400

ABOVE LEFT:
Steiff   9in(22.9cm) Dog(*)   1907
   White poodle cloth; gl. stickpin eyes;
   not jointed; (*)original red felt coat w/
   6 gold buttons & red felt slippers.
   No ID mark.   Excellent cond. $275

ABOVE RIGHT:
Steiff   10in(25.4cm) Bear(*)   c1907
   White mohair; gl. stickpin eyes; jtd.legs
   & arms; swivel head; straw stuffing;
   (*) block printed button in ear.
   Button.   Worn pads. $475

BELOW:
Steiff   11in(27.9cm) Bear(*)   1907
   Lt. brown mohair; shoe button eyes;
   swivel head; straw stuffing; (*)mounted
   on iron wheels 9in(22.9cm) high.
   Button in ear. Excellent cond. $350

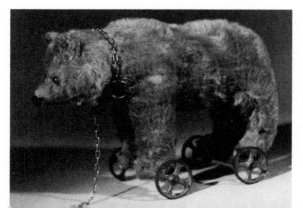

```
Steiff            12in(30.5cm) Bear         1907
   Tan mohair; shoe button eyes; jtd. legs &
   arms; straw stuffing.
   No ID mark.      Worn & soiled.        $250

Steiff            12in(30.5cm) Bear(*)      1907
   White mohair; shoe button eyes; swivel
   head; straw stuffing; (*)mounted on iron
   wheels; 10in(25.4cm) high.
   No ID mark.      Worn condition.       $400
BELOW:
Steiff            13in(31.8cm) Bear       c1907
   Cinnamon brown mohair (unusual color);
   shoe button eyes; jointed legs & arms;
   swivel head; straw stuffing.
   Button.          Worn/new pads.        $395
```

ABOVE RIGHT:
Steiff   13in(33.0cm) Bear   c1907
    Gold mohair; shoe button eyes; jtd. legs
    & arms; swivel head; straw stuffing.
    Button.   Worn condition. $450
ABOVE LEFT:
Steiff   13in(33.0cm) Bear   c1907
    Tan mohair; shoe button eyes; jtd. legs &
    arms; swivel head; straw stuffing.
    Button.   Worn condition. $450

ABOVE:

Steiff   15in(38.1cm) Bear   1907
    Gold mohair; shoe button eyes; jtd.legs
    & arms; swivel head; straw stuffing; but-
    ton on chest not original.
    No ID mark.   Slightly worn. $500

Steiff   13in(33.0cm) Bear   1907
    Tan mohair; shoe button eyes; jointed
    legs & arms; swivel head; straw stuffing;
    w/overalls similar to CHTB ill. 94.
    No ID mark.   Slightly worn. $475

Steiff   15in(38.1cm) Bear   1907
    Tan mohair; shoe button eyes; jtd. legs &
    arms; swivel head; straw stuffing; button
    on chest not original.
    No ID mark.   Slightly worn. $500

ABOVE LEFT:
Steiff   17in(43.2cm) Bear   1907
   Gold mohair; shoe button eyes; jointed
   legs & arms; swivel head; straw stuffing.
   No ID mark.   30% fur worn off. $350
ABOVE RIGHT:
Steiff   18in(45.7cm) Bear   1907
   Tan mohair; shoe button eyes; jointed
   legs & arms; swivel head; straw stuffing.
   Button in ear. Mint condition. $700

```
Steiff          26in(66.0cm) Bear          1907
   Gold mohair; shoe button eyes; jointed
   legs & arms; swivel head; straw stuffing.
   Button.          Mint condition.          $900

Steiff          9in(22.9cm) Bear          1908
   Reddish-brown mohair; shoe button eyes;
   jointed legs & arms; swivel head; straw
   stuffing.
   No ID mark.     20% fur missing.     $395

Steiff          9in(22.9cm) Bear          c1908
   Apricot mohair; shoe button eyes; jointed
   legs & arms; swivel head; straw stuffing.
   Rare size & color.
   Button.          Excellent cond.          $500

Steiff          10in(25.4cm) Bear          1908
   Gold mohair; shoe button eyes; jtd. legs
   & arms; swivel head; straw stuffing.
   Lg. plain but.  20% fur missing.     $300

Steiff          13in(33.0cm) Bear          c1908
   Gold mohair; shoe button eyes; jtd. legs
   & arms; swivel head; straw stuffing.
   Button          Excellent cond.          $550

Steiff          10in(25.4cm) Bear(*)     1910
   Tan mohair; shoe but. eyes; unjointed;
   swivel head; straw stuffing; (*)bear on
   wheels; "Appealing."
   No ID mark.     Poor condition.          $295

Steiff          10in(25.4cm) Bear(*)     1910
   Gold mohair; shoe button eyes; jtd. legs
   & arms; swivel head; (*)on wheels, has
   back & forth motion, squeaker. #192 CHTB.
   Button in ear.  Slightly worn.          $450

Steiff          10in(25.4cm) Bear(*)     1910
   Gold mohair; shoe but. eyes; jtd. legs &
   arms; sw. head; str. stuffing; (*)rides
   tricycle; "Steiff" embossed on wheels.
   Button in ear.  Excellent cond.          $500
```

ABOVE:
Steiff   12in(30.5cm) Bear   1910
   Tan mohair; shoe button eyes; jtd. legs &
   arms; swivel head; straw stuffing.
   No ID mark.   Worn; needs rep. $400

ABOVE:
Steiff   13in(33.0cm) Bear   c1910
   White mohair; shoe button eyes; jointed
   legs & arms; swivel head; straw stuffing.
   No ID mark.   Excellent cond. $550

ABOVE:
Steiff   14in(35.6cm) Bear   c1910
  Lt. brown mohair (scarce color); shoe
  button eyes; jtd. legs & arms; sw. head;
  straw stuffing.
  No ID mark.   Excellent cond. $450

Steiff   18in(44.5cm) Bear(*)   c1910
  Wht. mohair; shoe button eyes; jtd. legs
  & arms; sw. head; straw stuf; squeeker;
  (*) Withington Auction, July 1-2, 1983.
  Plain button.   Excellent cond. $1,260

```
Steiff              11in(27.9cm) Bear        c1920
    Gold mohair; shoe button eyes; jtd. legs
    & arms; swivel head; straw stuffing.
    No ID mark.      Fur ex. pads wrn.      $375

Steiff              9in(22.9cm) Bear(*)    c1930
    Lt. brown mohair w/ white nose; glass
    eyes; (*)hand puppet.
    No ID mark.      Worn condition.        $35
```

BELOW:
```
Steiff              9in(22.9cm) Bear(*)    c1930
    (*)Bear doll; tan mohair w/brown head,
    paws & feet; gl. eyes; jtd. legs & arms;
    sw. head; kapok stuff; flesh jersey body.
    Button.         Worn condition.         $90
```

ABOVE:
Steiff   14in(35.6cm) Bear   c1930
   "Teddy Baby"; gold mohair; glass eyes;
   jointed legs & arms; swivel head; straw
   stuffing.
   No ID mark.   Mint condition. $800

Steiff   9in(22.9cm) Bear(*)   1930
   "Jackie" 50th Ann. standing bear; gold
   mohair; glass eyes; jtd. legs & arms;
   swivel hd.; straw stuff; wht. stit. nose.
   Jubilee 1903-53
   Paper Tag/Butt. Mint condition. $800

Steiff   14in(35.6cm) Bear(*)   c1930
   (*)"Teddy Baby"; white plush; glass eyes;
   jtd. legs & arms; sw. head; str. stuff;
   2 but. on collar, 1 in ear; CHTB ill. 17.
   Buttons.   Slightly worn. $400

ABOVE:
Steiff   20in(50.8cm) Bear   c1930
   Gold mohair; shoe button eyes; jointed
   legs & arms; swivel head; straw stuffing.
   Button in ear. Mint condition. $800

Steiff   22in(55.9cm) Bear   c1930
   Pale gold mohair; glass eyes; jtd. legs &
   arms; swivel head; straw stuffing.
   No ID mark.   Excellent cond. $400

ABOVE LEFT:
Steiff   28in(71.1cm) Bear   c1930
   Lt. brown long mohair; shoe button eyes;
   jointed legs & arms; swivel head; straw
   stuffing.
   No ID mark.   Mint condition. $800
ABOVE RIGHT:
Steiff   10in(25.4cm) Bear   c1940
   White mohair; velvet nose & paws; glass
   eyes; jointed legs & arms; swivel head;
   straw stuffing.
   No ID mark.   30% fur missing. $200

Steiff   10in(25.4cm) Bear   c1940
   Gold mohair; glass eyes; jointed legs &
   arms; swivel head; str. stuffing.
   CHTB Ill. 22.
   Button.   Slightly worn. $300

Steiff   25in(63.5cm) Bear   c1940
    Gold mohair; shoe button eyes; jointed
    legs & arms; swivel head; straw stuffing.
    No ID mark.   Worn condition. $450

Steiff   3in(7.6cm) Bear(*)   1947
    Tan mohair; glass stickpin eyes; jointed
    legs & arms; swivel head; (*)made of
    metal.
    Tag US Zone Gr. Mint condition. $125

Steiff   10in(25.4cm) Bear   c1950
    Gold mohair; glass eyes; jointed legs &
    arms; swivel head; straw stuffing.
    No ID mark.   Excellent cond. $145

BELOW:
Steiff   9in(22.9cm) Bear   c1950
    Gold mohair; glass eyes; jointed legs &
    arms; swivel head; straw stuffing.
    No ID mark.   Fur ex./pads wrn. $145

```
Steiff            14in(35.6cm) Bear        c1950
   White plush; glass eyes; jointed legs &
   arms; swivel head; straw stuffing.
   CHTB Ill. 15.
   Button.         Worn condition.        $200
```

BELOW LEFT:
```
Steiff            11in(27.9cm) Bear        c1950
   Gold mohair; glass eyes; jointed legs &
   arms; swivel head; straw stuffing.
   No ID mark      Worn condition.        $195
```

BELOW RIGHT:
```
Steiff            22in(55.9cm) Bear        c1950
   Pale gold mohair; glass eyes; jtd. legs &
   arms; swivel head; straw stuffing.
   No ID mark.     Slightly worn.         $400
```

Steiff   20in(50.8cm) Bear   1954
    Dk.brown mohair; glass eyes; jointed legs
    & arms; swivel head; straw stuffing.
    Cl. Tag & But. Mint condition. $350

Steiff   3in(07.6cm) Bear   c1957
    Gold mohair; glass stickpin eyes; jointed
    legs & arms; swivel head; straw stuffing;
    tag reads "Original Teddy."
    Tag & button.   Excellent cond. $125

BELOW:
Steiff   5in(12.7cm) Bear   1957
    Tan mohair; glass eyes; swivel head;
    straw stuffing.
    Cl. Tag & But. Mint condition. $150

Steiff   6in(15.2cm) Bear   1957
   Gold mohair; glass eyes; jtd. legs & arms
   swivel head; straw stuffing.
   No ID mark.   Excellent cond. $135

Steiff   10in(25.4cm) Bear   1957
   White mohair; glass eyes; swivel head;
   straw stuffing.
   Cl. Tag & But. Mint condition. $350

Steiff   24in(61.0cm) Bear(*)   1957
   Caramel mohair; glass eyes; not jointed;
   straw stuffing; (*) mounted on four red
   disc wheels.
   Cl. Tag & But. Mint condition. $395

ABOVE LEFT:
Steiff   9in(22.9cm) Bear(*)   1958
   (*)"Orsi"; begging/sitting bear; tan mo-
   hair; glass eyes; jtd. arms; swivel head.
   No ID mark.   Excellent cond. $200

ABOVE RIGHT:
Steiff   17in(43.2cm) Bear   1958
   Gold mohair; glass eyes; jointed legs &
   arms; swivel head; straw stuffing.
   Cl. Tag & But. Mint condition. $275

OPPOSITE PAGE, ABOVE RIGHT:
Steiff   6in(15.2cm) Bear   c1959
   Gold mohair; glass eyes; jointed legs &
   arms; swivel head; straw stuffing.
   Tag & button.   Mint condition. $150

OPPOSITE PAGE, BELOW LEFT:
Steiff   9in(22.9cm) Bear(*)   1959
   Lt. brown mohair; tan felt pads; white
   nose; glass eyes; not jointed; straw
   stuffed head only; (*) hand puppet.
   No ID mark.   Worn condition $35

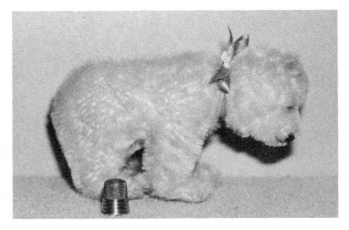

ABOVE:
Steiff   4in(10.2cm) Bear(*)   c1960
  White mohair; peach pads; glass stickpin
  eyes; swivel head; straw stuffing.
  (*) Standing Polar.
  No ID mark.   Excellent cond. $85

BELOW LEFT:
Steiff   6in(15.2cm) Bear   c1960
  Polar Bear standing; white mohair; claws
  painted on; plastic eyes; not jointed;
  straw stuffing; collar w/bell.
  Tag & button.   Mint condition. $95

BELOW RIGHT:
Steiff   7in(17.8cm) Bear   c1960
  Polar Bear standing; white mohair; felt
  pads w/stitched claws; plastic eyes; not
  jointed; straw stuffing; collar w/bell.
  Tag & button.   Mint condition. $140

ABOVE LEFT:
Steiff   6in(15.2cm) Bear(*)   c1960
   Tan mohair w/tan felt pads; glass eyes;
   sw. head; not jointed; standing position;
   (*) bell & paper tag on green collar.
   Paper tag.   Excellent cond. $95

ABOVE MIDDLE:
Steiff   7in(17.8cm) Bear   c1970
   Tan mohair w/ plush pads; plastic eyes;
   jtd. legs & arms; sw. head; straw stuf-
   fing.
   Tags & button. Mint condition. $125

ABOVE RIGHT:
Steiff   6in(15.2cm) Bear(*)   c1960
   Tan mohair; gl. eyes; swivel head; not
   jointed; straw stuffing; (*) bell & paper
   tag on green collar.
   Tags.   Excellent cond. $95

ABOVE LEFT:
Steiff   8in(20.3cm) Bear   c1960
   Gold mohair; glass eyes; jointed legs &
   arms; swivel head; straw stuffing; paper
   tag "51% wool, 49% cotton; St.Orig.Marke.
   Lbl.orig.teddy. Excellent cond. $100

ABOVE MIDDLE:
Unknown(German) 6in(15.2cm) Bear   c1950
   Tan mohair w/ open mouth; glass eyes;
   jtd. legs & arms; swivel head; straw
   stuffing; can stand.
   No ID mark.   Excellent cond. $225

ABOVE RIGHT:
Steiff   4in(10.2cm) Bear   1958
   Gold mohair; glass eyes; jointed legs &
   arms; swivel head; straw stuffing.
   Pap. tag & but. Mint condition. $95

Steiff   13in(33.0cm) Bear   c1960
    White mohair; glass eyes; jointed legs &
    arms; swivel head; straw stuffing.
    No ID marks.   Excellent cond. $125

BELOW RIGHT:
Steiff   6in(16.5cm) Bear(*)   c1960
    (*)"Zotty"; tan w/gold chest mohair;glass
    eyes; jointed legs & arms; swivel head;
    straw head & kapok body stuffing.
    Tag & button.   Excellent cond. $100

BELOW LEFT:
Steiff   7in(17.8cm) Bear(*)   1970
    (*)"Zotty"; lt. brown with gold chest
    mohair; glass eyes; jointed legs & arms;
    swivel head; straw stuffing.
    Button in ear.   Mint condition. $75

83

ABOVE:
Steiff   9in(22.8cm) Bear   c1970
  Tan mohair w/sheared face; glass eyes;
  jtd. legs & arms; swivel head;straw stuf-
  fing.
  Button / tag.   Mint condition. $75

84

ABOVE RIGHT:
Steiff   11in(27.9cm) Bear(*)   c1970
   (*) "Minkey-Zotty"; lt. brown imitation
   fur; plastic eyes; jtd. legs & arms; swi-
   vel head; foam rubber stuffing.
   Tags & button. Mint condition. $185

ABOVE LEFT:
Steiff   11in(27.9cm) Bear(*)   c1970
   (*) "Minky-Zotty"; beige imitation fur;
   plastic eyes; jtd. legs & arms; swivel
   head; foam rubber stuffing.
   Tags & button. Mint condition. $185

BELOW:
Steiff   15in(38.1cm) Bear(*)   c1970
   (*)Cozy Teddy." Lt. brown/white chest mo-
   hair & dacron; glass eyes; jointed legs &
   arms; swivel head; kapok stuffing."
   Paper tag.   Excellent cond. $125

ABOVE LEFT:
Steiff   12in(30.5cm) Bear(*)   c1970
   (*)"Cosy Teddy"; caramel Dralon & cotton
   fur w/ peach felt pads; plastic eyes; jtd
   legs & arms; swivel head.
   Tags & button. Mint condition. $100

ABOVE MIDDLE:
Steiff   12in(30.5cm) Bear(*)   c1970
   (*)"Cosy Teddy"; white Dralon & cotton
   fur; plastic eyes; jtd. legs & arms; sw.
   head; Dralon stuffing.
   Tags & button. Mint condition. $125

ABOVE RIGHT:
Steiff   12in(30.5cm) Bear(*)   c1970
   (*)"Cosy Teddy"; dk. brown Dralon & cot-
   ton fur; plastic eyes; jtd. legs & arms;
   Dralon stuffing.
   Tags & button. Mint condition. $100

Steiff   33in(83.8cm) Bear(*)   c1970
   (*)"Zotty"; lt. brown with gold chest
   mohair; glass eyes; jointed legs & arms;
   swivel head; straw stuffing.
   Button in ear. Mint condition. $600

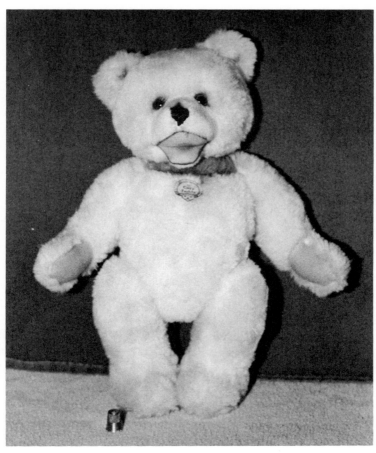

ABOVE:
Steiff   16in(40.6cm) Bear(*)   c1970
(*)"Cosy Teddy"; white Dralon & cotton w/
felt pads; glass eyes; jtd. legs & arms;
sw. head;open mouth of peach/orange felt.
Tags & button. Mint condition. $200

ABOVE:
Steiff   16in(40.6cm) Bear(*)   c1975
    Lt. brown "Fristed" mohair; glass eyes;
    jtd. legs & arms; sw. head; (*)pull
    string on side & bear says ten sentences.
    No ID mark.   Excellent cond. $300

ABOVE:
Steiff   11in(27.9cm) Bear(*)   c1977
    (*)"Zooby" w/open mouth; brown mohair;
    plastic eyes; jtd. arms; sw. head; straw
    stuffing; leather soles on large feet.
    Paper tag.   Mint condition. $300

ABOVE LEFT:
Steiff   17in(43.2cm) Rabbit(*) c1976
(*)German Olympic w/open mouth; red suit
& blue hat; tan Dralon & cotton; plastic
eyes; jtd. legs & arms; foam & wool stuf.
Tag & button.   Mint condition. $95

ABOVE MIDDLE:
Steiff   15in(38.1cm) Bear(*)   c1977
(*)"Zolac" humanized bear w/long legs;
lt. brn. chest; dk. brn. body; mohair;
glass eyes; jtd. legs & arms; str. stuff.
Tag & button.   Mint condition. $250

ABOVE RIGHT:
Steiff   15in(38.1cm) Rabbit(*) c1977
(*)"Lulac" humanized; lt. brn. chest,legs
& front feet; body darker; paws gold mo-
hair; gl. eyes; jtd. legs/arms; sw. head.
Tag & button.   Mint condition. $125

OPPOSITE PAGE, ABOVE RIGHT:
Steiff   24in(61.0cm) Bear(*)   1978
Caramel mohair; glass eyes; jtd. legs &
arms; swivel head; straw stuffing; (*)pa-
per tag reads "Orig Teddy."
Tags & button.   Mint condition. $300

OPPOSITE PAGE, BELOW LEFT·
Steiff   9in(22.9cm) Bear(*)   c1980
Tan Dralon & cotton fur w/ velvet pads;
plastic eyes; not jointed; wears orange
felt suit; (*)marionette w/ strings.
Tags & button.   Mint condition. $85

```
Steiff          17in(43.2cm) Bear          1980
    100th Ann. bear; gold mohair; shoe button
    eyes; jointed legs & arms; swivel head;
    Ltd. 5000 USA 6000 others; CHTB ill. 713.
    Ltd. Ed.
    Cloth tag/but.  Mint-in-box.          $350

Steiff          17in(43.2cm) Bear(*)       1980
    (*) 100th Anniversary Bear; gold mohair;
    black glass eyes; jtd. legs & arms; swiv-
    el head; excelsior stuf. CHTB Ill. 713.
    Ltd. Edition
    Tag & button    Mint-in-box.          $350
```

BELOW:
```
Steiff          11in(27.9cm) Bear(*)      c1981
    (*)"Lully"; lt. brn. mohair w/ wht. chest
    & tan paws; peach felt in open mouth;
    plastic eyes; not jointed; swivel head.
    Paper tag.      Mint condition.        $85
```

```
Steiff          14in(35.6cm) Bear(*)      1981
   (*)Anniversary Bears; Mother & Baby; gold
   mohair; shoe button eyes; jtd. legs/arms;
   swivel heads; CHTB Ill. 714
   Ltd. Ed. 8000.
   Cloth tags.     Mint-in-box.          $250
```

BELOW RIGHT:
```
Steiff          10in(25.4cm) Bear(*)      1983
   (*) "Margaret Strong" bear; gold mohair;
   plastic eyes; jtd. legs & arms; sw. head;
   foam & rubber stuffing.
   Tags & button.  Mint-in-box.           $50
```

BELOW LEFT:
```
Steiff          12in(30.5cm) Bear(*)      1983
   (*) "Margaret Strong" bear; gold mohair;
   plastic eyes; jtd. legs & arms; sw. head;
   rubber & foam stuffing.
   Tags & button.  Mint-in-box.           $65
```

LEFT TO RIGHT:

Steiff   2in(05.1cm) Bird(*)   c1950
   Yellow wool w/brown & green markings;
   glass stickpin eyes; swivel head; no
   stuffing; (*)movable metal feet & legs.
   Cloth tag/but. Mint condition. $15

Steiff   2in(05.1cm) Bird(*)   c1950
   Blue wool head, green wings & yellow bre-
   ast; gl. stickpin eyes; sw. head; no stuffing; felt beak & tail; (*)metal legs.
   Paper tag.   Mint condition. $15

Steiff   2in(05.8cm) Duck(*)   1950
   Blue, green, grey & white wool; glass
   stickpin on red felt eyes; felt beak; (*)
   metal movable legs & feet.
   No ID mark.   Mint condition. $20

Steiff   3in(07.6cm) Pidgeon   c1950
   White, blue & brown wool w/brown marking;
   glass stickpin eyes; swivel head; (*)met-
   al movable legs painted pink.
   No ID mark.   Excellent cond. $25

Steiff   3in(06.4cm) Duck(*)   c1950
   Green, blue, brown & white wool; glass
   stickpin on red felt eyes; sw. head; no
   stuffing; (*)large wht. wool tuft on hd.
   No ID mark.   Excellent cond. $20

Steiff   2in(05.1cm) Bird   c1950
   Coral chest w/gr. back wings w/dk. brown
   on wing tips 100% wool; gl. stkpin eyes;
   swivel head; "Geschuter 6508 Steiff orig"
   Paper tag/but. Mint condition. $20

Steiff   1in(02.5cm) Bird   c1955
    Wool tufts; olive back & wings; brown
    tail & tips; gray bill; no stuffing;metal
    legs & feet.
    Tag & button.   Excellent cond. $20

BELOW LEFT:
Steiff   6in(15.2cm) Bird(*)   1958
    (*)"Hucky"; raven; black mohair w/black
    felt wings & orange felt open bill; metal
    feet; gl. stickpin eyes; swivel head.
    Paper tag.   Mint condition. $100

BELOW RIGHT:
Steiff   4in(10.2cm) Bird(*)   1958
    (*)"Hucky"; Raven; black mohair w/black
    felt tail & orange felt open bill; metal
    feet; gl. stickpin eyes; swivel head.
    Paper tag.   Mint conditon. $95

ABOVE LEFT:
Steiff   4in(10.2cm) Parakeet c1977
   Yellow head & wings; green w/black marks;
   cot. velvet; glass stickpin eyes; foam,
   wool, cotton & rubber stuffing; "Hansi."
   Tag & button.   Mint condition. $75

ABOVE RIGHT:
Steiff   4in(10.2cm) Bird(*)   c1977
   (*)"Franzi"; Parakeet; wht. head w/ blue
   body & blk. markings; cot. velvet; glass
   stickpin eyes; foam, wool & rubber stuff.
   Tag & button.   Mint condition. $75

BELOW:
Steiff   8in(20.3cm) Boar(*)   c1976
   (*)"Dalle"; brown & white imitation fur;
   plastic tusks; plastic eyes; not jointed;
   foam stuffing.
   No ID mark.   Excellent cond. $100

Steiff   6in(15.2cm) Camel   1959
    Pale gold imi. fur w/ velvet legs & face;
    painted-on hooves; rope tail; plastic
    eyes; not jointed; straw stuffing.
    Tags & button. Excellent cond. $45

Steiff   51in   Carriage c1910
    Wooden carriage w/glass panels, lace cur-
    tains & metal rail at top; wooden wheels;
    doors open; coat of arms on doors.
    No ID mark.   Excellent cond. $1,000

ABOVE LEFT:
Steiff   5in(12.7cm) Dog   c1900
    Tan velvet w/brown ears; glass stickpin
    eyes; not jtd; straw stuffing; leather
    muzzle held by two plain Steiff buttons.
    Buttons.   Worn condition. $50

ABOVE MIDDLE:
Steiff   3in(07.6cm) Cat   c1900
    Tan mohair w/blk., green & gold marking;
    glass stickpin eyes; not jtd; str. stuff;
    orig. pink ribbon, bell & pink wool ball.
    Button (tiny). Soiled condition. $75

ABOVE RIGHT:
Steiff   6in(11.5cm) Duck   c1900
    Tan velvet w/blk. marks on wings; glass
    stickpin on red felt eyes; not jtd. straw
    stuff; green & gold scarf; hat.
    No ID mark.   Worn condition. $75

LEFT TO RIGHT:

Steiff   4in(10.2cm) Cat   c1960
   White mohair w/blk. markings; glass eyes;
   not jtd; swivel head; straw stuffing.
   Paper tag/but. Mint cond. $40

Steiff   4in(10.2cm) Cat   c1950
   White mohair w/black markings; glass eyes; jtd. legs & arms; sw. head; str. stu-
   fing; cl. label on leg "U.S. Zone Ger."
   Cloth label.   Excellent cond. $75

Steiff   4in(10.2cm) Cat(*)   c1960
   White mohair w/blk. markings; glass eyes;
   not jtd; straw stuffing; orig. tie w/
   bell; (*)standing.
   Paper tag/but. Mint condition. $35

Steiff   4in(10.2cm) Tiger Cub c1950
   Gold mohair w/blk. markings; white face,
   chest & paws; glass eyes; not jtd; swivel
   head; straw stuffing.
   No ID mark.   Excellent cond. $25

ABOVE:
Steiff   4in(10.2cm) Cat   c1900
    Tan & black velvet w/ orange markings on
    head & ears; gl. stickpin eyes; not jtd;
    pink ball of cotton tufts; straw stuff.
    Button.   Soiled & worn. $95

BELOW:
Steiff   9in(22.9cm) Cat   c1950
    White mohair w/blk. markings; glass eyes;
    jtd. legs & arms; sw. head; straw stuff-
    ing.
    Button.   Excellent cond. $125

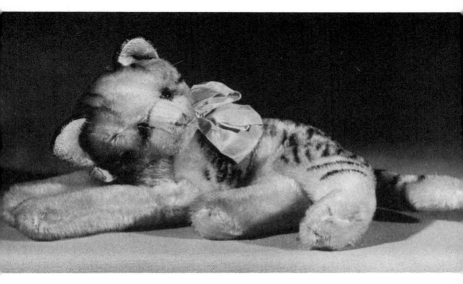

ABOVE:
Steiff   7in(17.8cm) Cat   c1960
    White mohair w/blk. markings; green
    glass eyes; not jtd; swivel head; straw
    stuffing.
    Paper tag/but.   Excellent cond. $85

Steiff   6in(15.2cm) Cat   c1970
    Black velvet w/blk. mohair tail; glass
    eyes; not jointed; straw stuffing.
    Paper tag/but.   Mint condition. $30

BELOW:
Steiff   3in(07.6cm) Cat(*)   1960
    (*) "Topsy"; white & gray mohair w/ black
    markings; green glass eyes; not jointed;
    straw stuffing; orig. ribbon w/ bell.
    Cloth tag.   Mint condition. $55

Steiff   4in(10.2cm) Cat   c1978
    Black cotton body; plastic eyes; not jtd;
    foam stuffing.
    Tags & button. Mint condition. $75
ABOVE RIGHT:
Steiff   10in(25.4cm) Cat   c1978
    Black mohair body; green plastic eyes;
    not jointed; swivel head; bristled tail;
    foam stuffing.
    Tags & button. Mint condition. $150

ABOVE:
Steiff   31in(78.7cm)   "Jocko"   1957
   Dark brown mohair; white whiskers; glass
   eyes; jointed legs & arms; swivel head.
   No ID mark.   Excellent cond. $700

Steiff   11in(27.9cm) Cock   1960
   Green,yellow, white, black,& orange mohair w/red felt comb & waddles; felt feet
   w/brn. marks; blk plastic eyes; str.stuf.
   Button on tail. Mint condition. $150

Steiff   13in(33.0cm) Dinosaur   c1955
    Vari-colored blue, green, violet & pink
    felt top; cream & black underbelly; glass
    eyes; not jointed; straw stuffing.
    No ID mark.   Excellent cond. $100

BELOW:
Steiff   5in(12.7cm) Cow   c1960
    Wht. mohair w/gold marks; white felt
    horns; wht. & blk. gl. eyes; not jtd;
    str. stuff; red leather collar/bell.
    Button.   Excellent cond $50

BELOW:
Steiff   6in(15.2cm) Cow(*)   1960
(*)"Bessy"; gold & white mohair; white
felt udders & horns; plastic eyes; not
jtd; straw stuff; cowbell & red neck band
Paper tag.   Mint condition. $95

BELOW LEFT:
Steiff   3in(07.6cm) Dog   c1950
    White mohair w/blk. spots; brown & black
    glass eyes; not jtd; straw stuffing; ori-
    ginal red ribbon & bell around neck.
    Paper tag/but. Excellent cond. $35

BELOW RIGHT:
Steiff   4in(10.2cm) Lamb   c1950
    Wht. mohair w/yellow marks; felt ears;
    green & blk. glass eyes; not jtd; straw
    stuffing; orig. red ribbon & bell.
    Paper tag/but. Mint condition. $35

Steiff   6in(15.2cm) Dog(*)   c1900
    Brown felt; glass eyes; not jointed;
    straw stuffed; (*)on red wheels.
    No ID mark.   Worn & repaired. $100

BELOW:
Steiff   17in(43.2cm) Dog   c1960
    Black mohair poodle; glass eyes; jtd.
    legs & arms; swivel head; straw stuffing.
    Button.   Mint condition. $100

Steiff   13in(33.0cm) Dog(*)   c1950
    Brown mohair; glass eyes; not jointed;
    cotton stuffing; (*)Dachshund.
    No ID mark.   Good condition. $52

Steiff   9in(22.9cm) Dog(*)   1957
    (*)"Waldi." Gold mohair head & frt. paws;
    cotton body; wears grn. felt hunter's
    suit; rifle missing.
    Button.   Excellent cond. $200

BELOW LEFT:
Steiff   13in(33.0cm) Dog(*)   c1950
    (*)"Molly"; white w/ brown mottling wool
    & cotton; glass eyes; swivel head; straw
    stuffing.
    Tag & button.   Excellent cond. $185

BELOW RIGHT:
Steiff   3in(07.6cm) Dog(*)   1959
    (*)"Foxy"; white mohair; glass eyes; not
    jointed; straw stuffing; collar w/ bell.
    Tag & button.   Excellent cond. $50

ABOVE LEFT:
Steiff   10in(25.4cm) Dog(*)   1959
   Long brown & white mohair (*) Cocker
   Spaniel w/ sheared nose; gl. eyes; swivel
   head; not jointed; straw stuffing.
   No ID mark.   Excellent cond. $200

ABOVE RIGHT:
Steiff   12in(30.5cm) Dog(*)   1959
   (*)"Arco" police dog; white & gray long
   mohair; glass eyes; swivel head; not
   jointed; straw stuffing; reclining pose.
   No ID mark.   Excellent cond. $200

BELOW:
Steiff   13in(33.0cm) Dog(*)   c1960
   White long mohair; shirred inner ears;
   glass eyes; swivel head; straw stuffing;
   (*) Red Steiff collar around neck.
   No ID mark.   Excellent cond. $175

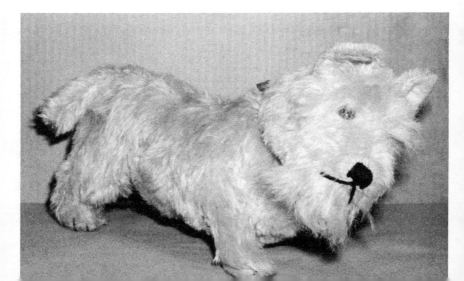

LEFT TO RIGHT:
Steiff   4in(10.2cm) Sheep(*)   1978
    (*)"Snucki"; white body w/black face,
    ears & feet of woven synthetic fur; plas-
    tic eyes; not jointed; foam, rubber stuf.
    Tags & button. Mint condition. $45

Steiff   4in(10.2cm) Lamb(*)   1978
    (*)"Flori"; white woven synthetic fur;
    plastic eyes; not jointed; wood foam
    stuffing.
    Tags & button. Mint condition. $35

Steiff   8in(20.3cm) Doll(*)   1978
    (*)"Vincenz"; black hat, pants & shoes;
    red shirt w/white sleeves; all of velvet
    (trevia); rubber-type face; painted eyes.
    Tags & button. Mint condition. $25

Steiff   4in(10.2cm) Dog(*)   1978
    (*)"Klaff"; lt. brown synthetic fur;
    plastic eyes; not jointed; foam rubber
    stuffing.
    Tags & button. Mint condition. $25

Steiff   4in(10.2cm) Dog(*)   1960
   (*)"Peky"; gold mohair; painted black
   nose, mouth & jowls, pink mouth; gl. eyes
   jtd. legs & arms; sw. head.
   Paper tag.   Mint condition. $75

ABOVE LEFT:
Steiff   5in(12.7cm) Donkey   c1910
   Tan velvet w/blk. mane; glass stickpin
   eyes; not jtd; str. stuffing; red leather
   straps w/plain buttons; red & blk. sadl.
   No ID mark.   Worn condition. $75
ABOVE RIGHT:
Steiff   5in(11.5cm) Donkey   c1910
   Tan velvet w/blk. mane; gl. stickpin ey-
   es; not jtd; str. stuff; braided cord
   tail; red floss brdl. w/gr. felt butns.
   Cloth tag/but. Worn condition. $100

Steiff   6in(15.2cm) Duck   1957
   Green head, white face & neck, brn. wings
   & rust chest mohair; lg. orange web feet;
   gl. stickpin eyes; not jtd; straw stuff.
   Paper tag.   Mint condition. $40

Steiff   6in(15.2cm) Duck   1957
    White mohair body, w/white felt tail,
    orange felt bill & large feet; gl. stick-
    pin eyes; not jtd; straw stuffing.
    No ID mark.   Excellent cond. $40

ABOVE:
Steiff   9in(22.9cm) Elephant   1958
    (*)"Jumbo"; gray mohair w/ gray pads &
    painted-on toes; peach in open mouth; gl.
    eyes; jtd. arms; sw. head; bell on trunk.
    No ID mark.   Excellent cond. $100

Steiff   4in(10.2cm) Elephant   1958
    Gray mohair, felt ears & pads; twisted
    cord tail; plastic eyes & tusks; not jtd;
    suede blanket w/ Steiff & bear head.
    Steiff blanket. Mint condition. $75

ABOVE LEFT:
Steiff   4in(10.2cm) Elephant c1977
   Gray mohair body; gray felt ears & paws;
   twisted string tail; trunk down; plastic
   eyes; not jtd.; wht. plastic tusks.
   Tag & button.   Mint condition. $35

ABOVE MIDDLE:
Steiff   7in(17.8cm) Elephant c1977
   Gray mohair w/red felt blanket w/two
   bells; plastic eyes; sw. head; wht. plas-
   tic tusks; painted on toes; straw stuff.
   Button.   Mint condition. $95

ABOVE RIGHT:
Steiff   7in(17.8cm) Elephant c1977
   Gray mohair w/gray felt pads & painted
   on toes; red felt bib; blk. stitched eyes
   recining(sleeping) position; foam stuff.
   Button.   Mint condition. $45

ABOVE RIGHT:
Steiff   8in(20.3cm) Elephant   c1977
    Sitting w/trunk up w/bell on end; open
    mouth; gray mohair; plastic eyes; not jtd
    sw. head; label on red bib says "Jumbo."
    Label.   Mint condition. $100

ABOVE LEFT:
Steiff   15in(38.1cm) Elephant   c1977
    Sitting w/trunk up; gray mohair; plastic
    eyes; jtd. arms; swivel head; foam rubber
    stuffing; label on red bib says "Jumbo."
    Tag & button.   Mint condition. $150

BELOW:
Steiff   9in(21.6cm) Fawn   c1960
   Tan w/white spots mohair; blk. glass
   eyes; not jtd; reclining 18in(45.7cm)
   long; original label.
   Paper tag/but. Mint condition. $175

ABOVE LEFT:
Steiff   3in(08.3cm) Frog   c1940
    Dk. green velvet w/blk. marks; gl. eyes;
    not jtd; straw stuffing; label on chest.
    Paper tag/but. Excellent cond. $50

ABOVE MIDDLE:
Steiff   5in(11.5cm) Walrus(*) c1950
    (*)"Paddy." Tan mohair w/brn. markings;
    wht. & blk. glass eyes; not jtd; straw
    stuffing; "Paddy" label on chest.
    Paper tag/but. Mint condition. $35

ABOVE RIGHT:
Steiff   5in(11.5cm) Pengn.(*) c1950
    (*)"Peggy." Wht. & blk. mohair tuxedo w/
    orange beak & feet; gl. eyes; not jtd;
    tag on chest reads "Peggy."
    Paper tag/but. Excellent cond. $45

ABOVE:
Steiff   16in(40.6cm) Giraf.(*) c1960
   (*)"Okapi." Baby giraffe; lt. brown
   mohair; w/blk. markings; glass eyes; not
   jointed; straw stuffing.
   Paper tag.   Mint. $195

Steiff   6in(15.2cm) Goat(*)   c1960
  (*)"Zicky." Tan mohair w/blk. markings.
  green gl. eyes w/blue pupils; not jtd;
  str. stuff; ribbon tied bell around neck.
  Paper tag.   Mint condition. $40

Steiff   4in(10.2cm) Hamster*   1960
  *"Goldy"; gold & white mohair w/ felt
  paws & pink inner ears; glass eyes; not
  jointed; straw stuffing.
  Tags & button. Mint condition. $50

ABOVE LEFT:
Steiff   5in(12.0cm) Hedgehog   1960
   (*)"Joggi"; long lt. brn. mohair back; w/
   short mohair front; pink felt ears; glass
   stkpn eyes; not jtd. sw. head; str. stuf.
   Tags & button. Mint condition. $50

ABOVE RIGHT:
Steiff   8in(20.3cm) Squirrel   1960
   (*)"Perri"; lt. brn. body; wht. felt paws
   wht. nylon thread nose & whiskers; black
   plastic & wht. felt eyes; swivel head.
   Tags & button. Mint condition. $150

Steiff   9in(22.9cm) Hen   1960
    White mohair w/black, orange & yellow
    markings; felt feet w/brown marking;
    black plastic eyes; straw stuffing.
    Button on tail. Mint condition. $150

Steiff   4in(10.2cm) Hen   1959
    Yellow bill; red comb & throat; white
    chest; gray edge on wings; white back
    mottled brown; tan felt tail; gl. eyes.
    No ID mark.   Mint conditon. $30

Steiff   22in(55.9cm) Horse(*) c1900
    Rust brown felt w/ white inner ears, nose
    & shins; black hooves; leather saddle &
    reins w/ metal stirrups; (*) on wheels.
    No ID mark.   Excellent cond. $500

Steiff   27in(68.6cm) Horse   c1910
    Tan mohair w/felt nostrils & horsehair
    mane & tail; brn. gl. eyes; not jointed;
    straw stuff; each horse valued at $600.
    Button.   Excellent cond. $2,400

Steiff   11in(27.9cm) Kangaroo c1960
    (*)"Kangoo"; gold & white mohair; black
    feet marking; plastic eyes; swivel head;
    straw stuffing; mother w/plastic baby.
    Two tags.   Mint condition. $75

OPPOSITE PAGE:
Steiff   15in(38.1cm) Koala   1950
    Lt. tan mohair; glass eyes; jointed legs
    & arms; swivel head; straw stuffing;
    scarce.
    No ID mark.   Excellent cond. $300

ABOVE:
Steiff   6in(15.2cm) Lion(*)   c1950
(*)"Leo." Gold w/brown mohair; glass
eyes; not jtd; straw stuff; reclining
10in(25.4cm) long.
Button.   Mint. $95

BELOW:
Steiff   8in(19.1cm) Lion(Cub)   1958
Yellow/brown spotted mohair; green glass
eyes (glows in dark); not jtd; straw
stuffing; reclining 14in(35.6cm) long.
Label missing. Excellent cond. $50

BELOW:
Steiff   11in(27.9cm) Llama   1957
  Spotted long hair plush; glass eyes; not
  jointed; straw stuffing; painted on
  hoofs.
  Tags & button. Mint condition. $200

ABOVE:
Steiff   22in(55.9cm) Monkey   c1910
    Brown mohair; felt hands & feet; glass
    eyes; jtd. legs & arms; long mohair tail.
    No ID mark.   Excellent cond. $300

Steiff   11in(27.9cm) Monkey   c1930
   Lt. brown mottled w/gold mohair; felt
   hands & feet w/stitched fingers & toes;
   gl. eyes; jtd. legs/arms; sw. hd; straw.
   No ID mark.   Worn condition. $100

Steiff   10in(25.4cm) Monkey(*)   1950
  (*)"Cocoli"; bellhop monkey w/red felt
  suit & black felt shoes; green & black
  glass eyes; sw. head; straw stuffing.
  Tags & button. Mint condition. $150

BELOW:
Steiff   15in(38.1cm) Monkey   1977
  Brown Dralon fur w/ made-on red troussers
  & felt paws; plastic eyes; not jointed;
  foam rubber, wool & cotton stuffing.
  Tags & button. Mint-in-box. $65

LEFT TO RIGHT:

Steiff   6in(15.2cm) Owl(*)   1960
  (*)"Wittle"; gold mohair w/wht. face; lg.
  green plastic eyes; sw. head; not jtd.;
  foam, cotton & rubber stuffing.
  Tag & button.   Mint condition. $100

Steiff   4in(10.2cm) Owl(*)   1960
  (*)"Wittie"; mottled tan & gold mohair;
  wht. felt feet; green & black plastic
  eyes; foam, cotton & rubber stuffing.
  Tag & button.   Mint condition. $75

Steiff   12in(30.5cm) Owl(*)   1960
  (*)"Wittie"; gold & white mohair; white
  felt feet; lg. green plastic eyes; foam,
  cotton & rubber stuffing.
  Tag & button.   Mint condition. $185

Steiff   9in(22.9cm) Owl(*)   1960
  (*)"Wittie"; tan, gold & green mohair;
  plastic eyes; sw. head; not jointed; foam
  cotton & rubber stuffing.
  Tag & button.   Mint condition. $145

ABOVE:
Steiff   6in(15.2cm) Panda   c1950
     Black & white mohair; glass eyes; jointed
     legs & arms; swivel head; straw stuffing;
     tag on chest "Steiff Original Mark Panda"
     Tag(see above). Mint condition. $95

Steiff   9in(22.9cm) Parrot(*)   1976
   (*)"Lora"; vari-colored mohair w/marked
   blue felt feet; glass eyes; swivel head;
   plastic beak; straw stuffing.
   Tag & button.   Mint condition. $185
BELOW:
Steiff   8in(20.3cm) Pidgeon   c1980
   Gray mohair; blue markings on felt wing
   tips; black shoe button eyes; not joint-
   ed; foam stuffing.
   Paper tag.   Mint condition. $75

ABOVE LEFT:
Steiff   3in(07.6cm) Pig   c1960
   Brown w/peach marking trevira velvet
   body; pink cord tail; glass stickpin
   eyes; not jointed; straw stuffing.
   Tag & button.   Mint condition. $50

ABOVE RIGHT:
Steiff   8in(20.3cm) Pig   c1960
   Rosey tan mohair w/mohair tail; black
   glass eyes; swivel head; straw stuffing;
   mouth open.
   No ID mark.   Excellent cond. $150

BELOW:
Steiff   6in(15.2cm) Rabbit   c1930
   Tan w/ brown spots velvet; glass stickpin
   eyes; not jointed; straw stuffing.
   No ID mark.   Soiled & worn. $35

ABOVE LEFT:
Steiff   9in(22.9cm) Rabbit(*)   1948
    Tan plush head & paws w/ tan cotton body;
    (*) dressed as a boy not original.
    Button.   Excellent cond. $85

ABOVE RIGHT:
Steiff   9in(22.9cm) Rabbit(*)   1948
    Tan plush head, ears & paws; tan cotton
    body; glass eyes; not jtd. sw. head; str.
    stuff; (*) cloth tag "U.S. Zone Germany."
    Tag & button.   All original. $100

ABOVE:

Steiff   9in(22.9cm) Rabbit   c1948
    Gold mohair w/ white front; glass eyes;
    swivel head; straw stuffing; sitting/beg-
    ging position; "Made in Germany."
    Tags & button. Excellent cond. $100

ABOVE:
Steiff   11in(27.9cm) Rabbit(*)   1948
Tan mohair head, feet & hands; gl. eyes;
swivel head; not jointed; straw stuffing;
(*) Humanized w/ blouse, skirt & apron.
Cloth tag.   Slightly worn. $95

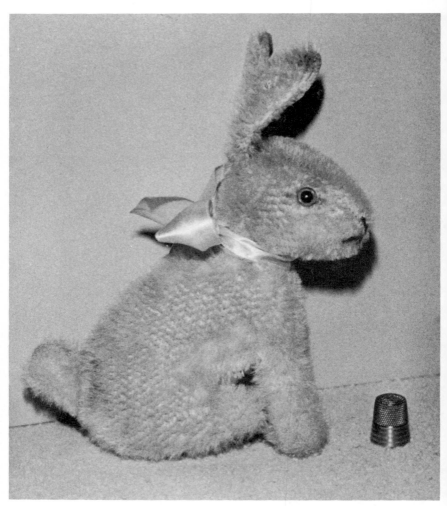

ABOVE:
Steiff 7in(17.8cm) Rabbit c1950
  Pale gold mohair w/ pink velvet inner
  ears; glass eyes; not jointed; straw
  stuffing; sitting position.
  No ID mark. Excellent cond. $100

Steiff 11in(27.9cm) Rabbit(*) c1950
  Mohair head, back of front paws & top of
  feet; cotton humanized body(*); glass
  eyes; not jtd; sw. head; Made In Germany.
  Tag U.S. Zone. Worn condition. $75

Steiff   13in(33.0cm) Rabbit(*) c1950
    Tan mohair; glass eyes; jtd. legs & arms;
    swivel head; straw stuffing; original
    ribbon around neck; (*)standing.
    Button.   Excellent cond. $125

ABOVE:
Steiff   14in(35.6cm) Rabbit(*) c1950
    Pale gold mohair w/wht. front; glass
    eyes; not jtd; sw. head; (*)standing.
    Button.   Excellent cond. $95

ABOVE:
Steiff   23in(58.4cm) Rabbit(*) c1950
  Lt. brown w/wht. face & chest; glass
  eyes; jtd. arms; sw. head; str. stuffing;
  (*)sitting/begging position.
  Button.   Excellent cond. $200

ABOVE:
Steiff   12in(30.5cm) Rabbit(*)   1951
    Pale gold mohair; glass eyes; jtd. legs &
    arms; sw. head; str. stuff; (*)pull toy
    on red wheels.
    Cl. tag/pap.lb. Excellent cond. $125

BELOW LEFT:
Steiff   6in(15.2cm) Rabbit(*)   1957
    Brown & white mohair; pink velvet ears;
    glass eyes; bell around neck; (*)running
    rabbit.
    Tags & button.   Excellent cond. $135

BELOW MIDDLE:
Steiff   7in(17.8cm) Rabbit(*)   1957
    Brown & white mohair; pink velvet ears;
    glass eyes; not jointed; straw stuffing;
    bell on ribbon around neck; (*)running.
    Tag & button.   Excellent cond. $150

BELOW RIGHT:
Steiff   3in(07.6cm) Rabbit(*)   1957
    Brown & white mohair; glass eyes; not
    jointed; straw stuffing; (*)running
    rabbit.
    Tag & button.   Excellent cond. $85

```
Steiff            6in(15.2cm) Rabbit      1957
   Standing; tan mohair w/ white front;glass
   eyes; not jointed; swivel head.
   Clot tag & but. Slightly worn.        $50

Steiff           10in(25.4cm) Rabbit(*)  1957
   (*)"Varlo"; shaded lt. brown & white
   mohair; gl. eyes; jtd. legs; swivel head;
   "Running, sitting, begging, rabbit."
   Tags & button.  Mint condition.       $125
```

BELOW:
```
Steiff            6in(15.2cm) Rabbit      1958
   Gold mohair w/ white front; glass eyes;
   swivel head; not jointed; straw stuffing;
   sitting position.
   No ID mark.      Excellent cond.       $100
```

ABOVE:
Steiff   18in(45.7cm) Rabbit   1958
   Tan mohair w/ white front; glass eyes;
   swivel head; not jointed; straw stuffing;
   sitting/begging position.
   Button w/script Mint condition. $200

Steiff   3in(07.6cm) Rabbit   1959
    Running; gold mohair w/ wht. face & paws;
    glass eyes; not jointed; paper tag on
    chest reads "Orig. Steiff." Ribbon & bell
    Paper tag.   Excellent cond. $50

BELOW:
Steiff   8in(20.3cm) Rabbit(*)   1959
    (*)"Cozy" Mummy; lt. brown mohair body;
    white chest, tail, soles of feet, face, &
    inside ears; gl. eyes; not jtd.
    No ID mark.   Excellent cond. $45

ABOVE:
Steiff   13in(33.0cm) Rabbit   c1965
   Brown & white mohair; white whiskers;
   glass eyes; jtd. arms; swivel head; straw
   stuffing.
   No ID mark.   Excellent cond. $200

Steiff   18in(45.7cm) Rabbit   c1960
   White & beige mohair; tan felt pads; pink
   embroidered nose; white whiskers; glass
   eyes; jtd. arms; sw. head; straw stuff.
   No ID mark.   Mint condition. $200

ABOVE LEFT:
Steiff   23in(58.4cm) Rabbit(*) c1970
(*)"Ossi"; lt. brown synthetic fur; not
jointed; swivel head; synthetic stuffing.
Tags & button. Mint condition. $60

ABOVE MIDDLE:
Steiff   18in(45.7cm) Rabbit(*) c1970
(*)"Ossi"; lt. brown body w/white chest &
ears; glass eyes; not jointed; synthetic
stuffing.
Tags & button. Mint condition. $40

ABOVE RIGHT:
Steiff   23in(58.4cm) Rabbit(*) c1970
(*)"Ossi"; lt. brown synthetic fur w/
white face, chest & inner ears; pink em-
bossed nose; gl. eyes; sw. head; not jtd.
Tags & button. Mint condition. $60

Steiff   16in(40.6cm) Rabbit   1977
   (*)"Lulac"; tan mohair;plastic eyes; not
   jointed; foam, rubber, wool & cotton
   stuffing.
   Tags & button. Mint-in-box. $65

ABOVE:
Steiff   7in(17.8cm) Ram(*)   c1960
  (*)"Snucki." Long wht. & short blk. mo-
  hair; blk. markings on horns; green &
  blue eyes; not jtd; straw stuffing.
  Paper tag.   Mint condition. $45

Steiff   10in(25.4cm) Reindeer   c1950
    White mohair w/gold & brown markings; tan
    felt antlers; glass eyes; not jointed;
    straw stuff; Steiff santa not valued.
    Tag & button.   Excellent cond. $85

Steiff   4in(10.2cm) Rooster   1959
    Yellow bill; green, orange, yellow &
    brown mottled body; green felt tail; gl.
    eyes; sw. head; painted red metal feet.
    No ID mark.   Mint condition. $30

ABOVE:
Steiff   9in(22.9cm) Tiger   c1950
    Gold mohair w/black stripes & white ch-
    est; green glass glow-in-dark eyes; not
    jointed; straw stuff. four teeth open mo.
    Button.   Excellent cond. $150

Steiff   12in(29.2cm) Tiger   c1970
    Gold w/stripes mohair; glass eyes (glows
    in dark); not jtd; wool, foam & rubber
    stuffing.
    Paper tag/but. Mint condition. $200

Steiff   3in(07.6cm) Turkey   c1950
    Wool tufts in white & green w/ brown mar-
    kings; glass stickpin eyes; swivel head;
    movable metal legs painted pink.
    No ID mark.   Excellent cond. $25

Steiff   5in(12.0cm) Turkey   c1958
    Brown, green & white mottled mohair body
    w/ red head, bill & wadoles; felt tail &
    wings; gl. stickpin eyes; metal feet.
    No ID mark.   Excellent cond. $50

BELOW:
Steiff   6in(15.2cm) Turtle   1957
    Yellow & brown mohair; rubber shell; gl.
    stickpin eyes; not jointed; straw stuff-
    ing.
    But. on shell. Worn condition. $25

ABOVE:

Steiff   12in(30.5cm) Turtle(*) c1977
   (*)"Slo"; mottled green & brown mohair;
   open mouth; glass eyes; not jointed;
   straw stuffing; felt claws.
   Button.   Mint condition. $100

Strauss   14in(35.6cm) Bear(*)   1906
   Tan plush; shoe button eyes; jointed legs
   & arms; swivel head; straw stuffing.
   (*)Has crank operated music box.
   Paper tag.   Worn condition. $400

OPPOSITE PAGE, ABOVE:

Unknown   22in(55.9cm) Bear(*)   c1880
   Lt. reddish brown mohair w/papier mache
   body; realistic glass eyes; not jointed;
   (*)bear nods & breathes; stands 13in hi.
   No ID mark.   Excel.works well. $1,500

BELOW:
Unknown   12in(30.5cm) Bear   c1903
    Gold mohair; shoe button eyes; jtd. legs
    & arms; swivel head; straw stuffing;
    sailor cap & brown jug not original.
    No ID mark.   Excellent cond. $350

ABOVE:
Unknown   18in(45.7cm) Bear(*)   c1890
    White mohair; realistic glass eyes; not
    jointed; (*) German clock works key-wind;
    stands on papier mache ice berg; nods hd.
    No ID mark.   Excellent cond. $1,500

Unknown (Ger.?) 14in(35.6cm) Bear   c1907
    Tan mohair; shoe button eyes; jointed
    legs & arms; swivel head; straw stuffing.
    No ID mark.   40% fur missing. $195

BELOW:
Unknown   17in(43.2cm) Bear   c1907
    Tan mohair; painted black metal eyes;
    jointed legs & arms; straw stuffing.
    No ID mark.   Excellent cond. $500

Unknown   10in(25.4cm) Bear(*)   1908
    White cotton flannel; shoe button eyes;
    jtd. legs & arms; swivel head; str. stuf-
    fing. (*)Sold by Butler Bros.
    No ID mark.   Worn condition. $75

BELOW:
Unknown (Ger.)   15in(38.1cm) Bear   c1908
    Tan mohair; shoe button eyes; jointed
    legs & arms; swivel head; straw stuffing.
    No ID mark.   Excellent cond. $350

ABOVE:
Unknown   13in(33.0cm) Bear   c1910
    Tan wool (no fur); shoe button eyes; jtd.
    legs & arms; swivel head; straw stuffing;
    clothes not original.
    No ID mark.   Worn condition. $150

Unknown   8in(20.3cm) Bear   c1910
    Face wht. mohair; wht. felt pads & feet;
    sleeves, hood & dress wine-red wool wors-
    ted; CHTB ill. 381A & B.
    No ID mark.   Good condition. $95

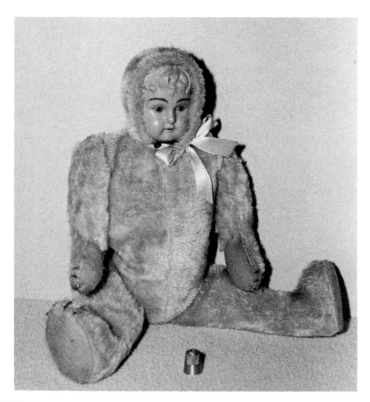

ABOVE:

Unknown   16in(40.6cm) Bear(*)   1910
Lt. grey mohair; ptd. eyes & face;jointed
lgs. & arms; sw. head; str. stuff;.(*)
Teddy Doll celluloid face; sold by Sears.
No ID mark.   Excellent cond. $250

Unknown   14in(35.0cm) Bear   c1910
Tan mohair w/ tan felt pads; shoe button
eyes; jtd. legs & arms; swivel head;straw
stuffing.
No ID mark.   Excellent cond. $300

Unknown   15in(38.1cm) Bear   c1910
Long curley black mohair (scarce color);
glass eyes; jointed legs & arms; swivel
head; straw stuffing.
No ID mark.   Mint condition. $500

Unknown(Ideal?) 20in(50.8cm) Bear   c1910
   Gold mohair w/ black fabric nose; painted
   metal eyes; jtd. legs & arms; sw. head;
   straw stuffing.
   No ID mark.   Excellent cond. $350

BELOW:
Unknown (Eng.)   23in(58.4cm) Bear   c1910
   Gold mohair; shoe button eyes; jointed
   legs & arms; swivel head; nose is solid
   piece black cloth.
   No ID mark.   Excellent cond. $150

Unknown   25in(63.5cm) Bear   c1910
   Reddish-brown mohair w/ tan felt pads;
   blk. stitched nose; jtd. legs & arms; sw.
   head.
   No ID mark.   Excellent cond. $200

ABOVE LEFT:
Unknown (Amer.) 12in(30.5cm) Bear   c1930
   Long gold mohair; glass eyes; jointed
   legs & arms; swivel head; straw stuffing.
   No ID mark.   Mint condition. $135

ABOVE RIGHT:
Unknown   12in(30.5cm) Bear   c1912
   Gold mohair w/felt pads;shoe button eyes;
   jointed legs & arms; swivel head with
   extra-long nose; straw stuffing.
   No ID mark.   Slightly worn. $250

Unknown   7in(17.8cm) Bear(*)   c1914
    White long mohair; glass eyes; jtd. legs
    & arms; swivel head; straw stuffing.
    (*)Has sweet bisque face.
    No ID mark.   Mint condition. $250

Unknown   7in(17.8cm) Bear(*)   c1914
    Tan flannel plush; glass eyes; jtd. legs
    & arms; straw stuffing. (*)Has bisque
    Armand Marsielle doll face.
    No ID mark.   Excellent cond. $250

Unknown (Germ.) 7in(17.8cm) Bear(*)   c1914
    (*) Teddy Bear doll; tan flannel plush;
    wht. felt feet, hands & bonnet trim; brn.
    glass eyes; jtd. legs & arms; sw. head.
    No ID mark.   Excellent cond. $250

Unknown   7in(17.8cm) Bear(*)   1914
    Gold plush; shoe button eyes; not joint-
    ed; straw stuffing. (*)Mounted on wheels;
    has muzzle; CHTB ill. 188.
    No ID mark.   Worn condition. $350

Unknown   20in(50.8cm) Bear(*)   1914
    (*)"Electron"; eyes light up; tan mohair
    (also red, green & blue); elec. bulb eyes
    which light by pressing stomach.
    No ID mark.   Worn condition. $275

OPPOSITE PAGE:
Unknown   17in(43.2cm) Bear(*)   c1914
    Gold mohair; glass & shoe but. eyes; jtd.
    legs & arms; sw. head; str. stuf;(*)two-
    faced. CHTB Ill. 24 ABC
    No ID mark.   Worn condition. $1,000

Unknown   3in(07.6cm) Bear   c1915
   White cotton wadding over pressed sawdust
   body; black glitter eyes; not jtd.; red
   chenille poinsetia; metal rope; wood seat
   No ID mark;   Worn condition. $40

ABOVE:
Unknown 13in(33.0cm) Bear(*) c1915
   Dk. brown mohair; shoe button eyes; not
   jointed; straw stuffing. (*)21 inches
   (55.9cm) long.
   No ID mark.   Good condition. $600

BELOW:
Unknown 17in(43.2cm) Bear c1915
   Gold mohair; shoe button eyes; jtd. legs
   & arms; swivel head; straw stuffing.
   No ID mark.   Worn condition. $250

ABOVE LEFT:
Unknown (Japan)   5in(12.0cm) Bear   c1920
   Bright gold mohair; celluloid eyes; join-
   ted legs & arms; swivel head; straw stuf-
   fing; paper address & greeting tag.
   No ID mark.   Excellent cond. $40

ABOVE RIGHT:
Unknown (Japan)   5in(12.0cm) Bear   c1920
   Gold mohair; gl. stickpin eyes; jointed
   legs & arms; swivel head; straw stuffing;
   paper greeting tag w/poem & address.
   No ID mark.   Excellent cond. $40

Unknown   11in(27.9cm) Bear   c1920
   Gold mohair; glass eyes; jointed legs &
   arms; swivel head; straw stuffing; not
   much shape to feet.
   No ID mark.   Good/excel. cond. $125

OPPOSITE PAGE:
Unknown   32in(81.3cm) Bear   c1920
   Lt. brown mohair; shoe button eyes; jtd.
   legs & arms; swivel head; straw stuffing.
   No ID mark.   Excellent cond. $600

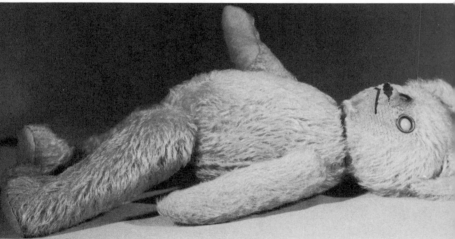

ABOVE:
Unknown   17in(43.2cm) Bear(*)   c1923
   Tan mohair; celluloid open/shut sleep
   eyes(*); jtd. legs & arms; swivel head;
   straw stuffing.
No ID mark.   Excellent cond. $500

Unknown   10in(22.3cm) Bear(*)   1923
   Tan plush head & hands; felt clothes; glass eyes; not jtd.; (*)metal body frame;
   walks or skates; imptd by Butler Bros.
   No ID mark.   Mint condition. $200

ABOVE:
Unknown (Germ.) 15in(38.1cm) Bear   c1925
   Gold mohair; shoe button eyes; jtd. legs
   & arms; swivel head; straw stuffing.
   No ID mark.   Worn condition. $200

Unknown(German) 19in(48.3cm) Bear(*)   c1925
   Long, curly white mohair; off-white felt
   pads; (*)pink velvet open/close mouth;
   gl. eyes; jtd. legs & arms; swivel head.
   No ID mark.   Excellent cond. $300

Unknown   16in(40.6cm) Bear(*)   1926
   Black backing gold mohair; sh. but. eyes;
   jtd. legs & arms; sw. head; str. stuff.
   (*)Mounted on red disc wheels.
No ID mark.   Worn condition. $375

Unknown (Japan)   5in(12.7cm) Bear   c1930
   Gold mohair; glass stickpin eyes; jointed
   legs & arms; swivel head; straw stuffing.
No ID mark.   Excellent cond. $75

Unknown   5in(12.7cm) Bear(*)   1930
   (*)"Winnie the Pooh" type; rust mohair;
   glass stickpin eyes; jointed legs & arms;
   straw stuffing.
No ID mark.   Good to excel. $100

ABOVE:
Unknown (Japan)   5in(12.7cm) Bear(*)   c1930
  Lt. brown w/wht. nose & pads; glass eyes;
  metal nose; not jointed; plush over metal
  frame; (*) walking bear.
No ID mark.   Mint condition. $35

ABOVE LEFT:
Unknown (Japan)   7in(17.8cm) Bear(*)   c1930
   Lt. brown plush; glass stickpin eyes;
   jointed legs & arms; swivel head; plush
   covers mechanism; bear performs & bows.
   No ID mark.   Excellent cond. $125

ABOVE RIGHT:
Unknown (Japan)   7in(17.8cm) Bear(*)   c1930
   Lt. brown plush on beer can body; glass
   stickpin eyes; jtd. legs & arms; swivel
   head; (*)wind-up to perform on trapeze.
   No ID mark.   Excellent cond. $125

Unknown   8in(19.1cm) Bear(*)   c1930
   Red mohair; glass stickpin eyes; jointed
   legs & arms; straw stuffing. (*)Has humanized felt face.
   No ID mark.   Worn condition. $95

170

BELOW:
Unknown   9in(22.9cm) Bear(*)   c1930
   Maroon plush; glass stickpin eyes; not
   jointed; pressed wood body has wind-up
   mechanism; moves arms & legs,opens mouth.
   No ID mark.   Mint condition. $200

ABOVE:
Unknown   10in(25.4cm) Bear   c1930
   Gold mohair; felt pads; glass "Googly"
   eyes looking to side; jtd. legs & arms;
   swivel head; straw stuffing.
   No ID mark.   Good-excel. cond. $150

ABOVE:
Unknown   10in(25.4cm) Bear(*)   c1930
   Lt. brown plush; gl. stickpin side-glanc-
   ing eyes; not jointed; (*)key wind-up in
   back plays instrument & moves head.
   No ID mark.   Excellent cond. $200

ABOVE:
Unknown   12in(30.5cm) Bear(*)   c1930
   Gold mohair over papier mache body; glass
   eyes; not jtd. (*)pull toy, red wdn. std;
   metal whls;red collar & muzzle trappings.
   No ID mark.   Excellent cond. $250

Unknown   13in(33.0cm) Bear(*)   c1930
   White extra long mohair; oversized glass
   eyes; jtd. legs & arms; swivel head;
   straw stuffing; (*)squeeze-music box.
   No ID mark.   Worn condition. $150

Unknown   15in(38.1cm) Bear   c1930
   Gold plush; shoe button eyes; jtd. legs &
   arms; swivel head; straw stuffing.
   CHTB Ill. 16.
   No ID mark.   Good condition. $150

Unknown   15in(38.1cm) Bear(*)   c1930
   Long curly blue plush; glass eyes; jointed arms; straw stuffing; (*) key-wind box
   in torso; bear walks & growls.
   No ID mark.   Mint condition. $800

ABOVE:
Unknown   14in(35.6cm) Bear(*)   1930
  (*)First edition "Winnie the Pooh"; dist.
by Woodnough, N.Y. Gold mohair; shoe but-
ton eyes; jtd. legs & arms; sw.hd. straw.
No ID mark.   Excellent cond. $400

ABOVE:
Unknown   16in(40.6cm) Bear   c1930
    Tan mohair; tan felt pads; very long
    arms; gl. eyes w/felt lids; jtd. legs &
    arms; sw. head; red felt tongue.
    No ID mark.   Repaired pads. $350

Unknown   17in(43.2cm) Bear   c1930
    White mohair; blue glass eyes (unusual);
    jtd. legs & arms; swivel head; straw
    stuffing.
    No ID mark.   Excellent cond. $300

Unknown   18in(45.7cm) Bear   c1930
   White mohair; shoe button eyes; jointed
   legs & arms; swivel head.
   No ID mark.   Good condition. $95

Unknown   18in(45.7cm) Bear   c1930
   White mohair; glass eyes; jointed legs &
   arms; swivel head; straw stuffing.
   No ID mark.   Excellent cond. $285

Unknown   19in(48.3cm) Bear(*)   c1930
   Cinnamon plush; glass eyes; not jointed;
   (*)Riding bear with metal handle for
   pushing child on bear.
   No ID mark.   2 wheels missing. $395

ABOVE:
Unknown   20in(50.8cm) Bear(*)   c1930
    Long gold mohair; shoe button eyes; jtd.
    legs & arms; sw. head; straw stuffing;
    (*)plays music when sides are squeezed.
    No ID mark.   Excellent cond. $400

Unknown   16in(40.6cm) Bear(*)   1931
   Dk. brown plush; glass eyes; not jointed;
   straw stuffing. (*)Riding bear on red
   disc wheels.CHTB Ill. 249
   No ID mark.   Good condition. $400

Unknown (Ger.)   12in(30.5cm) Bear(*)   1932
   Wht. mohair; glass eyes; jointed legs &
   arms; sw. head; kapok stuffing. (*)Wind-
   up music box plays "Rock-A-Bye Baby."
   No ID mark.   Mint condition. $95

Unknown (Japan) 3in(7.6cm) Bear(*)   c1935
   Lt. brown (*)ceramic; painted;
   CHTB Ill. 493.
   No ID mark.   Mint condition. $10

BELOW:
Unknown (Japan) 3in(9.6cm) Bear   c1936
   Gold plush over metal frame; painted met-
   al eyes & nose; looks like tape measure
   bear, but plain.
   No ID mark.   Mint condition. $35

Unknown   12in(30.5cm) Bear(*)   1936
    Tan plush; glass eyes; jtd. legs & arms;
    Kapok stuffing; (*)made in Australia;
    CHTB ill. 261.
    No ID mark.   Worn condition. $75

Unknown (Amer.) 18in(45.7cm) Bear   1936
    Gold mohair; glass eyes; jointed legs &
    arms; swivel head; straw stuffing.
    No ID mark.   Worn condition. $225
BELOW:
Unknown   18in(45.7cm) Bear(*)   1937
    (*)"Feed Me". Rust plush; black glass
    eyes; not jointed; straw in head. (*)Met-
    al box catches feed. CHTB Ill. 267.
    No ID mark.   Excellent cond. $125

ABOVE:
Unknown(France) 19in(45.7cm) Bear   c1939
   Off white lamb's wool; glass eyes; joint-
   ed legs & arms; straw head; kapok stuff-
   ing.
No ID mark.   Repaired cond. $125

Unknown   10in(25.4cm) Bear   c1940
   Gold mohair; glass eyes; jointed legs &
   arms; swivel head; cotton stuffing.
No ID mark.   Worn condition. $75

BELOW:
Unknown   12in(30.5cm) Bear   c1940
   Gold mohair; glass eyes; jointed legs &
   arms; swivel head; straw stuffing.
   No ID mark.   Worn condition. $65

ABOVE:
Unknown   13in(33.0cm) Bear   c1940
    Blue mohair; shoe button eyes; jointed
    legs & arms; swivel head; cotton stuffed.
    No ID mark.   Worn condition. $75

Unknown (Amer.) 14in(35.6cm) Bear   c1940
  White mohair; shoe button eyes; jointed
  legs & arms; swivel head; straw stuffing.
  No ID mark.   Excellent cond. $45

Unknown   14in(35.6cm) Bear(*)   c1940
  Tan plush; cowboy clothes part of bear.
  glass eyes; not jointed; kapok stuffing.
  CHTB ill. 80.
  No ID mark.   Mint condition. $45

Unknown (Amer.) 15in(38.1cm) Bear   1940
  Pink plush; glass eyes; not jointed;
  cotton stuffing. CHTB Ill. 273
  No ID mark.   Good condition. $20

Unknown   15in(38.1cm) Bear   c1940
  White mohair; glass eyes; jointed legs &
  arms; swivel head; straw stuffing. Bake-
  lite nose.
  No ID mark.   Mint condition. $165

Unknown (Japan) 16in(40.6cm) Bear(*)   c1940
  Reddish-gold plush; lg.blk.pupil w/small
  red iris; jtd. legs/arms; swivel head;
  (*)trans. radio; grumpy face; ptd. toes..
  No ID mark.   Excellent cond. $95

Unknown (Amer.) 18in(45.7cm) Bear   c1940
  Rust-red mohair; shoe button eyes; jointed legs & arms; swivel head; kapok stuffing.
  No ID mark.   Good-excel. cond. $225

Unknown   25in(63.5cm) Bear   c1940
  Tan mohair; glass eyes; jointed legs &
  arms; swivel head; straw stuffing.
  No ID mark.   Excellent cond. $295

ABOVE:
Unknown (U.S.A) 18in(45.7cm) Bear   c1940
   Gold mohair w/tan felt paws; metal nose;
   glass eyes; jtd. legs & arms; swivel
   head; straw stuffing; CHTB ill. 399.
   No ID mark.   Excellent cond. $250

ABOVE:
Unknown (Eng.)   26in(66.0cm) Bear   c1940
    Gold mohair; glass eyes; jointed legs &
    arms; swivel head; kapok stuffing.
    No ID mark.   Excellent cond. $325

BELOW:
Unknown (Ger.)   5in(11.5cm) Bear(*)   c1945
    Gold plush; gl. stickpin eyes; jtd. legs/
    arms; str.stuff.;head/arms/legs kapok bo-
    dy; (*)on 3-wheel metal tricycle; USzone.
    U.S. Zone mark. Mint condition. $150

Unknown (Japan) 6in(15.2cm) Bear(*) c1945
   White fake fur body w/metal glasses,
   knitting needles & chair; plastic eyes;
   metal frame body; marked "Made In Japan."
   Made In Japan. Excellent cond. $65

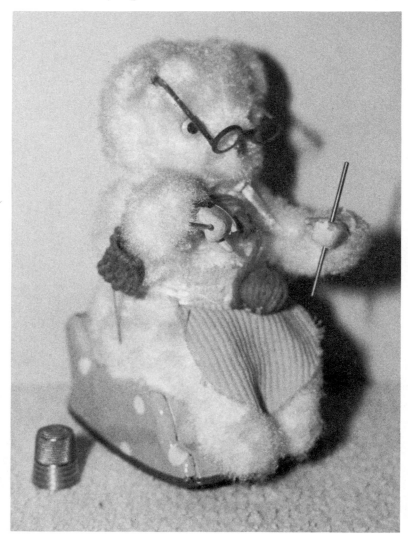

Unknown   22in(55.9cm) Bear   1945
   Face, arms & legs made of tan sheepskin;
   wears sewed-on leather overalls; glass
   eyes; not jointed; kapok stuffing.
   No ID mark.   Mint condition. $35

ABOVE LEFT:
Unknown (Germ.)   8in(20.3cm) Bear(*)   c1950
   Lt. brown mohair; glass eyes; jtd. legs &
   arms; straw stuffing; (*)tag reads "Ger-
   many East."
   Paper tag.   Mint condition. $45

ABOVE RIGHT:
Unknown (Germ.)   7in(17.8cm) Bear(*)   c1950
   Lt. brown mohair; glass eyes; jtd. legs &
   arms; straw stuffing; (*) tag reads "Ger-
   many East."
   Paper tag.   Mint condition. $40

Unknown (Swiss)   8in(20.3cm) Bear(*)   c1950
   White head & feet w/blue mohair body;
   peach felt paws; gl. eyes; not jointed;
   (*)rattle in paws; CHTB ill. 346.
   No ID mark.   Excellent cond. $125

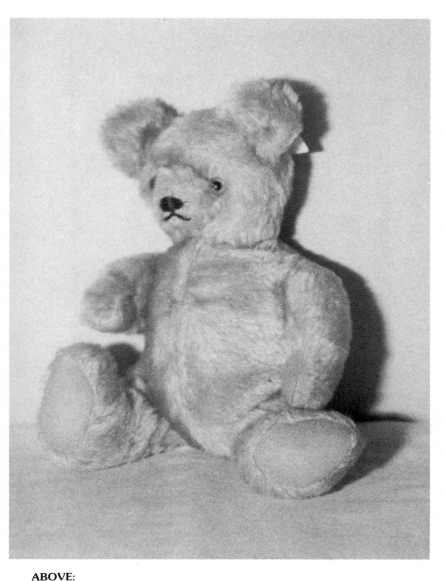

ABOVE:
Unknown (Ger.)   9in(22.9cm) Bear   c1950
    Lt. tan mohair; glass eyes; jointed legs
    & arms; swivel head; cotton stuffing.
    No ID mark.   Excellent cond. $50

ABOVE:

Unknown(German) 14in(35.6cm) Bear   c1950
    Lt. tan wooly mohair; short nose; glass
    eyes;jtd. legs & arms; swivel head; straw
    stuffing.
    No ID mark.   Excellent cond. $225

Unknown   19in(48.3cm) Bear   c1950
    Rust cotton string w/ white sewn-on nose;
    glass eyes; jtd. legs & arms; sw. head;
    cotton stuffing.
    No ID mark.   Worn condition. $40

BELOW:
Unknown (Ger.)   5in(12.7cm) Bear   c1960
    White plush; plastic eyes; jointed legs &
    arms; straw stuffed; ribbon across chest
    reads "Berlin."
    Ribbon.   Excellent cond. $50

BELOW:

Unknown   14in(35.6cm) Bear   c1960
    Long black mohair; plastic nose & eyes;
    jointed legs & arms; straw stuffed; rib-
    bon reads "Gruss aus Berlin."
    Ribbon tag.   Excellent cond. $160

Unknown (Japan)   4in(10.2cm) Bear(*)   c1970
   (*)"Smokey" salt shakers;#brown ceramic;
   painted clothes & features; $7.50 each.
   No ID mark.   Mint condition. $15

BELOW:
Unknown(Taiwan) 20in(50.8cm) Bear(*)   1977
   Gold synthetic mohair; red T shirt reads
   "Avon"; sales incentive for salesmen;
   plastic eyes; (*)Pan-Dee (importers).
   Label on shirt. Mint condition. $50

ABOVE:
Unknown (Ger.)   19in(48.3cm) Bear(*)   1979
    Lt. brown syn. mohair; plastic eyes; jtd.
    legs & arms; sw. head; styrofoam stuffing
    (*)sings & speaks in German.
    Has paper tag. Mint condition. $85

ABOVE:
Unknown (China)   8in(20.3cm) Bear   c1980
 Tan wool; plastic eyes; jtd. legs & arms;
 swivel head; straw stuffing; cl. tag says
 "Pure Wool" w/ Chines characters.
 Cloth tag.   Mint condition. $10

ABOVE:
Unknown (Korea) 11in(27.9cm) Bear(*)   1983
     Lt. brown w/white muzzle & ears; black
     plastic nose & eyes; blue "Dodgers" T
     shirt; (*)Dist. by Calif. Stuffed Toys.
     Cloth label.   Mint condition. $15

ABOVE:
Unknown   12in(30.5cm) Camel   c1880
    Tan w/black curly fur over papier mache
    body; glass eyes; not jointed.
    No ID mark.   Good condition. $75

BELOW:
Unknown   10in(25.4cm) Cat   c1930
   Long white mohair; large glass eyes; not
   jtd; swivel head; straw stuffing; possi-
   bly "Merry Thought."
   No ID mark.   Excellent cond. $150

ABOVE:
Unknown   15in(38.1cm) Cat   c1965
  Tan plush w/ black tail, ears & mouth;
  green plastic eyes; not jointed; kapok
  stuffing; sitting position.
  No ID mark.   Excellent cond. $25

201

BELOW:
Unknown (Ger.)   10in(25.4cm) Cat(*)   c1914
    Dark grey wool fabric over papier mache
    body; glass eyes; (*)pull string & cat's
    mouth opens & "meows."
    No ID mark.   Worn condition. $150

ABOVE:
Unknown   13in(30.5cm) Dog   c1945
   Long, curly white mohair w/ brown ears &
   tan pads; brown felt nose; red felt in
   open mouth; blk. stitched eyes; not jtd.
   No ID mark.   Excellent cond. $55

ABOVE LEFT:
Unknown   12in(30.5cm) Dog(*)   c1910
    White plush w/long white fur around face
    & tail; glass stickpin eyes; not jointed;
    straw stuffing; (*)large Afghan hound.
    No ID mark.   Good condition. $75

ABOVE RIGHT:
Unknown   9in(22.9cm) Dog(*)   c1910
    White plush w/long white fur around head
    & tail; shoe button eyes; not jointed;
    straw stuffing; (*)small Afghan hound.
    No ID mark.   Worn condition. $50

OPPOSITE PAGE, ABOVE:
Unknown (Japan) 10in(25.4cm) Dog(*)   c1960
    White plush w/long syn. fur on ears, tip
    of tail, head & legs; plastic eyes;
    (*)Poodle w/transistor radio inside.
    "H" within dia. Mint condition. $150

OPPOSITE PAGE, BELOW:
Unknown (Ger.) 14in(35.6cm) Horse(*)   c1880
    Twin horses; white w/lt. brown spots fur
    (horse hide) over papier & wood body; gl-
    ass eyes; (*)Pull toy on base w/wheels.
    No ID mark.   Good condition. $500

ABOVE:
Unknown (Ger.)   7in(17.8cm) Horse(*)   c1890
    Light brown plush over hard body; glass
    stickpin eyes; not jointed; (*)Pull toy
    on base w/wheels.
    No ID mark.   Mint condition. $165

BELOW:
Unknown (Ger.)   16in(40.6cm) Horse(*)   c1890
    Black wool over papier mache & wood body;
    glass eyes; not jointed; (*)Pull toy on
    base w/wheels.
    No ID mark.   Good condition. $125

Unknown   24in(61.0cm) Horse(*)   c1940
   Lt. brown imitation leather w/ brown ears
   & black mane; red leather halter, reins &
   saddle; metal stirrups; (*) on wheels.
   No ID mark.   Excellent cond. $300

BELOW:
Unknown   17in(43.2cm) Koala   c1935
   Lt. brown real fur w/ hard rubber nose;
   glass eyes; jtd. legs & arms; swivel head
   & straw stuffing.
   No ID mark.   Worn condition. $65

Unknown   16in(40.6cm) Koala   c1935
    Tan fur (possibly real kangaroo) w/ lea-
    ther nose & claws; glass eyes; not jtd;
    straw stuffing.
No ID mark.   Worn condition. $85

ABOVE:
Unknown (USA?)   10in(25.4cm) Monkey   c1940
    Lt. brown mohair w/ felt face & paws &
    white whiskers; gl. stickpin eyes; not
    jointed; tag reads "Mohair Character."
    Cloth tag.   Worn condition. $20

Unknown(Japan)   9in(22.9cm) Possum(*) c1909
    (*)"Billy Possum; gold plush w/ gold vel-
    vet inner ears; blk. glass eyes;not join-
    ted; blk. bead nose; stitched mouth.
    No ID mark.   Mint condition. $150

Unknown (German) 15in (38.1cm) Rabbit (*) c1907
  Lt. brown w/ tan inner ears, nose & eyes;
  glass eyes; not jointed; painted papier
  mache; (*) candy container.
  No ID mark.   Excellent cond. $150

Unknown (German) 13in (33.0cm) Rabbit (*) c1907
  White w/ black spots painted papier mache
  w/ glass eyes; (*) candy container w/ re-
  movable head.
  No ID mark.   Excellent cond. $150

Unknown   9in (22.9cm) Rabbit (*) c1936
  Painted wood & cardboard on wheels.
  (*) Pull toy.
  No ID mark.   Excellent cond. $25

ABOVE:
Unknown   12in(30.5cm) Ram   c1880
    Curly lamb's wool fur over papier mache &
    wood body; glass eyes; not jtd; horns pa-
    inted black over cloth covered armature.
    No ID mark.   Good condition. $150

OPPOSITE PAGE, ABOVE:
Wilkinson Mfg.   16in(40.6cm) Bear(*)   1981
    White acrylic fur; plastic eyes & nose;
    not jointed; tee shirt reads "Cruise On A
    Love Boat"; button "Princess Cruise."
    Button.   Mint condition. $25

Related Items

Bubbs-Merrill   11in(27.9cm) Related   1909
   Book: "Mother Goose's Teddy Bears" by
   Frederick L. Cavally, Jr. Bubbs-Merrill &
   Co. Publishers.
   Bubbs-Merrill. Excellent cond. $50

ABOVE:
D & C, N.Y.   25in(63.5cm) Related   1912
   Teddy Roosevelt campaign kerchief; red w/
   white design on cotton; reads: "Progress-
   ive Roosevelt 1912 Battle Flag."
   Printed initial Excellent cond. $100

Donahue & Co.   13in(33.0cm) Related   1907
    Book: "The Browns, A Book of Bears."Vers-
    es by B. Parker; Illus. by H. Parker;
    Published by M. A. Donahue & Co. Chicago.
    Donahue & Co.   Excellent cond. $50

BELOW LEFT:
Wm. Rogers Co.   6in(15.2cm) Related   c1970
    Silverplated souvenir spoon w/ bust of
    Theodore Roosevelt at top of handle; Pan-
    ama Canal view in bowl.
    Wm. Rogers Co.   Mint condition. $35

BELOW RIGHT:
Durgin Silver   6in(15.2cm) Related   c1907
    Sterling silver souvenir spoon; horse &
    Rough Rider at top; bust of T. Roosevelt
    below w/ crossed guns below; engr. bowl.
    "D" hallmark.   Excellent cond. $75

Edw. Stern & Co 11in(27.9cm) Related   1907
    Book: "More About Teddy B. & Teddy G.,
    The Roosevelt Bears" by Seymour Eaton.
    Stern & Co.   Excellent cond. $95

ABOVE:
Edward Sharp.   9in(22.9cm) Related   c1940
    Tin cookie container w/picture of little
    boy & Teddy Bear on cover; 6 gold bears
    around picture; Edward Sharp & Son, Ltd.
    Ed.Sharp & Sons Excellent cond. $45

Esmond   36in(91.4cm) Related   c1920
    Crib blanket; blue & white cotton revers-
    ible with bear picture printed on blan-
    ket.
    No. ID mark.   Mint condition. $50

Forbes Silver   3in(07.6cm) Related   c1915
    Baby cup,silverplated; marked "Forbes
    Silver Co. Quadruple Plate; three antique
    bears in swings in relief.
    Forbes Silver.   Excellent cond. $100

Goebel   3in(07.6cm) Related   c1970
    Bear salt & Bee Hive pepper shakers; cer-
    amic, painted in natural colors; has
    Goebel mark & "W. Germany."
    Goebel mark.   Excellent cond. $20

Ottmann Litho.   10in(25.4cm) Related   c1907
   Paper doll: Bear w/ 3 costumes- Naval,
   dress clothes & bathrobe. Envelope reads:
   "Teddy Bear Paper Doll" pub. J. Ottmann.
   Ottmann Litho.   Excellent cond. $75

Raphael Tuck   12in(30.5cm) Related   c1909
   Teddy Bear paper valentine with verse on
   back; jtd. legs & arms.
   Trademark.   Mint condition. $50

Saalfield Pub.   15in(38.1cm) Related   1937
   Book "The Three Bear Cut-Outs," Book
   #2142; colored punch-out pictures; standing house of 3 bears in centerfold.
   Saafield Pub.   Good condition. $25

BELOW:
Schmidt & Co.   8in(20.3cm) Related   1903
   Cigar box liner advertising "The Big Baer
   Cigar"; shows bruin holding a large cigar
   in forest setting; w/ "Bear This In Mind"
   Name on print.   Excellent cond. $20

Nisbet   8in(20.3cm) Related   1983
   Teddy Roosevelt doll in Rough Rider cos-
   tume holding brown bear. Limited Edition
   of 7,500 pieces.
   Ltd. Ed. 7,500.
   Paper tag.   Mint-in-box. $75

BELOW:
Schoenhut   8in(20.3cm) Related   1908
   Teddy Roosevelt figure made of jointed
   wood w/kahki hunting outfit; figure holds
   1905 bear.
   No ID mark.   Mint condition. $450

ABOVE:
Steiff   15in(38.1cm) Relat.(*) c1977
   Lady Bug footstool; mohair in natural
   colors of blue, white & red; metal frame;
   gl. eyes; foam stuff.; (*)"Cosy Crabby."
   Tag & button.   Mint condition. $100

Sherman Clay   12in(30.5cm) Related   1922
   Sheet music "Teddy Bear Blues," words &
   music by James H. Jackson; printed in
   blue & gold on white paper.
   Shermay Clay.   Excellent cond. $20

Steiff   4in(10.2cm) Related   1953
   "Fifty Years of Steiff" booklet w/ "Jackie" bear on cover celebrating Steiff's
   50th anniversary; story & color photos.
   Tag on cover.   Excellent cond. $20

Steiff   6in(15.2cm) Related   1958
   Booklet:"Theodore Roosevelt and the Teddy
   bear." Celebrating the 100th birthday of
   Theodore Roosevelt. Story & pictures.
   Steiff.   Mint condition. $20

Stella Olsen   Adult size   Related   1978
    Umbrella painted with white & brown bears
    and "Teddy Bear" words; nylon fabric;
    CHTB Ill. 469.
    C.Stella Olsen. Mint condition. $100

Unknown (Germ.)   Related   1907
    Child's china tea set (15 pcs.) decorated
    w/ scenes from "The Busy Bears" Book;
    refer to CHTB Ill. 615.
    No ID mark.   Excellent cond. $550

ABOVE:
Unknown (Amer.)   7in(17.8cm) Related   1907
    Milk glass souvenir plate w/ 3 bears in
    relief at top; center bear reading book;
    plate may be hung by a ribbon.
    No ID mark.   Excellent cond. $35

ABOVE:
Unknown   10in(25.4cm) Related   1907
   Cast iron bank; Teddy Roosevelt shoots
   coin into tree trunk, bear's head appears
   out of trunk; refer CHTB Ill. 687.
   No ID mark.   Good condition. $200

Unknown   2 yr. old.   Related   1907
   Child's coat made of gold mohair; 6 brass
   buttons with standing bears on them; buttons alone $15 each.
   No ID mark.   Worn condition. $100

OPPOSITE PAGE LEFT:
Unknown   2in(05.1cm) Related   c1950
   Sterling silver pendant of seated Teddy
   Bear; marked "Sterling."
   No ID mark.   Mint condition. $85

OPPOSITE PAGE MIDDLE:
Unknown (Eng.)   4in(10.2cm) Related   1910
   Sterling silver baby rattle w/ ivory
   teething stick for handle; English hall-
   arks.
   Eng. hallmarks. Excellent cond. $150

OPPOSITE PAGE RIGHT:
Unknown   2in(05.1cm) Related   1927
   Sterling silver & colored enamel pendant
   of Teddy Bear w/ ball in paw.
   No ID mark.   Mind condition $100

ABOVE LEFT:
Unknown   7in(17.8cm) Related   c1910
  Cast iron still bank, painted black w/
  red tongue; bear holds container for in-
  serting coin.
  No ID mark.   Excellent cond. $125

ABOVE RIGHT:
Unknown   5in(12.7cm) Related   c1940
  Still bank made of aluminum painted dark
  brown; standing bear.
  No ID mark.   Worn condition. $35

Unknown   8in(20.3cm) Related   1927
   Calendar; "Teddy Bear", for 1927;complete
   & in mint condition.
   No ID mark.   Mint condition. $25

Unknown (Japan)   Related   c1930
   Child's china tea set (15pcs.) w/ color-
   ful decoration of "Goldilocks & Three
   Bears" in gold,blue green & red.
   "Japan"   Mint condition. $250

BELOW:
Unknown   3in(07.6cm) Related   c1930
   Salt & pepper shakers; clear glass w/
   amber glass heads; priced as a pair.
   No ID mark. $25

ABOVE:

Unknown   7in(17.8cm) Related   c1930
   Bookends; aluminum painted black; bear is
   standing on all four legs.
   No ID mark.   Excellent cond. $15

Unknown (Japan) 3in(7.6cm) Related   c1930
   Gold plush; painted metal eyes & nose;
   jointed legs & arms; (*)metal frame con-
   tains tape measure; tag-Made In Japan.
   Orange oval tg. Mint condition. $50

Unknown (Germ.) 4in(10.2cm) Related   c1930
   Flatware (Knives, forks & spoons) 18 pcs.
   made of aluminum w/ embossed Teddy Bear
   on handles; original black case.
   Germany   Excellent cond. $150

Unknown   12in(30.5cm) Related   c1930
    Muff; two-faced; white mohair; bear face
    shoe but. eyes; doll face ptd. celluloid;
    sw. head; sateen lined; CHTB ill. 466A.
    No ID mark.   Excellent cond. $150

Unknown   10in(25.4cm) Related   1935
    Color photo print of Theodore Roosevelt,
    framed & dated 1935. Cloth tag reads
    "Born 1858-Died 1919."
    No ID mark.   Mint condition. $25

225

Index
Animal

Alli. (*)	Steiff	12in (30.5cm)	1957 - 51
Bear (*)	Aetna	12in (30.5cm)	1907 - 17
Bear (*)	Aetna	14in (35.6cm)	c1906 - 17
Bear (*)	American Char.	12in (30.5cm)	c1970 - 17
Bear (*)	Bluine Mfg.	10in (25.4cm)	1915 - 18
Bear	Bruin Mfg. Co.	12in (30.5cm)	1926 - 18
Bear	Bruin Mfg. Co.	13in (33.0cm)	1907 - 18
Bear	Chad Valley	13in (33.0cm)	c1950 - 19
Bear	Chad Valley	14in (35.6cm)	c1940 - 19
Bear	Chad Valley	19in (45.7cm)	c1930 - 18
Bear (*)	Charm Co. Korea	13in (31.8cm)	c1980 - 20
Bear (*)	Columbia T B Mf	17in (43.2cm)	1907 - 20
Bear (*)	Dakin	8in (20.3cm)	1979 - 21
Bear (*)	Dakin	18in (45.7cm)	1979 - 21
Bear (*)	Dakin	21in (53.3cm)	1980 - 21
Bear (*)	Dakin	22in (55.9cm)	1979 - 21
Bear (*)	Deetz	16in (40.6cm)	1977 - 21
Bear (*)	G.C. Gillespie	16in (40.6cm)	1907 - 22
Bear (*)	Geb. Sussenguth	14in (35.6cm)	c1925 - 22
Bear (*)	Geb. Sussenguth	14in (35.6cm)	c1925 - 22
Bear (*)	Grisley Marke	15in (38.1cm)	c1949 - 22
Bear (*)	Hermann	16in (40.6cm)	c1930 - 22
Bear	Hermann	20in (50.8cm)	c1950 - 24
Bear (*)	Ideal	11in (27.9cm)	1945 - 28
Bear (*)	Ideal	12in (30.5cm)	1981 - 31
Bear (*)	Ideal	15in (38.1cm)	1945 - 28
Bear (*)	Ideal	15in (38.1cm)	1978 - 30
Bear	Ideal	16in (40.6cm)	1924 - 28
Bear (*)	Ideal	16in (40.6cm)	1953 - 28
Bear (*)	Ideal	20in (50.8cm)	1954 - 28
Bear	Ideal	21in (53.3cm)	1945 - 28
Bear	Ideal	23in (58.4cm)	1910 - 26
Bear (*)	Ideal	23in (58.4cm)	1945 - 28
Bear	Ideal	24in (61.0cm)	c1900 - 25
Bear	Ideal	24in (61.0cm)	1910 - 27
Bear	Ideal	24in (61.0cm)	1920 - 27
Bear	Kersa	11in (27.9cm)	c1930 - 32
Bear	Knickerbocker	6in (15.2cm)	c1940 - 35
Bear	Knickerbocker	13in (33.0cm)	1940 - 35
Bear	Knickerbocker	14in (35.6cm)	c1950 - 35
Bear	Knickerbocker	14in (35.6cm)	c1960 - 35
Bear	Knickerbocker	16in (40.6cm)	c1930 - 33
Bear	Knickerbocker	17in (43.2cm)	c1930 - 33
Bear	Knickerbocker	26in (66.0cm)	c1930 - 34

Bear	Knickerbocker	40in (91.6cm)	c1939 - 34
Bear (*)	M.C.Z. (Swiss)	9in (22.9cm)	c1960 - 36
Bear (*)	Nisbet	18in (45.7cm)	1980 - 39
Bear	Petz	4in (10.2cm)	1930 - 39
Bear (*)	R.D. France	11in (27.9cm)	c1895 - 40
Bear (*)	R.D. France	15in (38.1cm)	c1930 - 40
Bear (*)	Rose Mary Orig.	16in (40.6cm)	1953 - 42
Bear (*)	Rushton Co.	12in (30.5cm)	c1977 - 43
Bear (*)	Schuco	4in (10.2cm)	c1930 - 46
Bear	Schuco	4in (10.2cm)	c1930 - 46
Bear	Schuco	4in (10.2cm)	c1930 - 46
Bear	Schuco	4in (10.2cm)	c1930 - 46
Bear (*)	Schuco	4in (10.2cm)	c1950 - 48
Bear (*)	Schuco	5in (12.7cm)	c1930 - 46
Bear (*)	Schuco	5in (12.7cm)	c1930 - 46
Bear (*)	Schuco	9in (22.9cm)	c1949 - 48
Bear	Schuco	11in (27.9cm)	1923 - 43
Bear (*)	Schuco	11in (27.9cm)	1926 - 44
Bear (*)	Schuco	17in (43.2cm)	1926 - 45
Bear (*)	Schuco	17in (43.2cm)	c1930 - 48
Bear	Shackman	3in (7.6cm)	c1930 - 50
Bear (*)	Steiff	3in (7.6cm)	1947 - 74
Bear	Steiff	3in (7.6cm)	c1957 - 76
Bear	Steiff	4in (10.2cm)	1905 - 51
Bear	Steiff	4in (10.2cm)	1905 - 51
Bear	Steiff	4in (10.2cm)	1958 - 82
Bear (*)	Steiff	4in (10.2cm)	c1960 - 80
Bear	Steiff	5in (12.7cm)	1907 - 58
Bear (*)	Steiff	5in (12.7cm)	c1907 - 59
Bear	Steiff	5in (12.7cm)	1957 - 76
Bear	Steiff	6in (15.2cm)	1907 - 59
Bear	Steiff	6in (15.2cm)	1908 - 58
Bear	Steiff	6in (15.2cm)	1957 - 77
Bear	Steiff	6in (15.2cm)	c1959 - 78
Bear	Steiff	6in (15.2cm)	c1960 - 80
Bear (*)	Steiff	6in (15.2cm)	c1960 - 81
Bear (*)	Steiff	6in (15.2cm)	c1960 - 81
Bear (*)	Steiff	6in (15.2cm)	c1960 - 83
Bear	Steiff	7in (17.8cm)	1907 - 58
Bear	Steiff	7in (17.8cm)	c1960 - 80
Bear (*)	Steiff	7in (17.8cm)	1970 - 83
Bear	Steiff	7in (17.8cm)	c1970 - 81
Bear	Steiff	8in (20.3cm)	1907 - 59
Bear	Steiff	8in (20.3cm)	c1960 - 82
Bear	Steiff	9in (22.9cm)	1905 - 52
Bear	Steiff	9in (22.9cm)	1908 - 66
Bear	Steiff	9in (22.9cm)	c1908 - 66
Bear (*)	Steiff	9in (22.9cm)	c1930 - 70

Bear (*)	Steiff	9in (22.9cm)	c1930 - 70
Bear (*)	Steiff	9in (22.9cm)	1930 - 71
Bear	Steiff	9in (22.9cm)	c1950 - 74
Bear (*)	Steiff	9in (22.9cm)	1958 - 78
Bear (*)	Steiff	9in (22.9cm)	1959 - 78
Bear	Steiff	9in (22.9cm)	c1970 - 84
Bear (*)	Steiff	9in (22.9cm)	c1980 - 90
Bear	Steiff	10in (25.4cm)	1907 - 60
Bear (*)	Steiff	10in (25.4cm)	c1907 - 61
Bear	Steiff	10in (25.4cm)	1908 - 66
Bear (*)	Steiff	10in (25.4cm)	1910 - 66
Bear (*)	Steiff	10in (25.4cm)	1910 - 66
Bear (*)	Steiff	10in (25.4cm)	1910 - 66
Bear	Steiff	10in (25.4cm)	c1940 - 73
Bear	Steiff	10in (25.4cm)	c1940 - 73
Bear	Steiff	10in (25.4cm)	c1950 - 74
Bear	Steiff	10in (25.4cm)	1957 - 77
Bear (*)	Steiff	10in (25.4cm)	1983 - 93
Bear (*)	Steiff	11in (27.9cm)	1907 - 61
Bear	Steiff	11in (27.9cm)	c1920 - 70
Bear	Steiff	11in (27.9cm)	c1950 - 75
Bear (*)	Steiff	11in (27.9cm)	c1970 - 85
Bear (*)	Steiff	11in (27.9cm)	c1970 - 85
Bear (*)	Steiff	11in (27.9cm)	c1977 - 89
Bear (*)	Steiff	11in (27.9cm)	c1981 - 92
Bear	Steiff	12in (30.5cm)	1903 - 53
Bear	Steiff	12in (30.5cm)	1907 - 62
Bear (*)	Steiff	12in (30.5cm)	1907 - 62
Bear	Steiff	12in (30.5cm)	1910 - 67
Bear	Steiff	12in (30.5cm)	c1920 - 53
Bear (*)	Steiff	12in (30.5cm)	c1970 - 86
Bear (*)	Steiff	12in (30.5cm)	c1970 - 86
Bear (*)	Steiff	12in (30.5cm)	c1970 - 86
Bear (*)	Steiff	12in (30.5cm)	1983 - 93
Bear	Steiff	13in (31.8cm)	c1907 - 62
Bear	Steiff	13in (31.8cm)	c1907 - 63
Bear	Steiff	13in (31.8cm)	c1907 - 63
Bear	Steiff	13in (31.8cm)	1907 - 64
Bear	Steiff	13in (31.8cm)	c1908 - 66
Bear	Steiff	13in (31.8cm)	c1910 - 68
Bear	Steiff	13in (31.8cm)	c1960 - 83
Bear	Steiff	14in (35.6cm)	c1910 - 69
Bear (*)	Steiff	14in (35.6cm)	c1930 - 71
Bear	Steiff	14in (35.6cm)	c1930 - 71
Bear	Steiff	14in (35.6cm)	1940 - 53
Bear	Steiff	14in (35.6cm)	c1950 - 75
Bear (*)	Steiff	14in (35.6cm)	1981 - 93
Bear	Steiff	15in (38.1cm)	1905 - 53

Bear	Steiff	15in (38.1cm)	1905 - 52
Bear	Steiff	15in (38.1cm)	1905 - 54
Bear	Steiff	15in (38.1cm)	1907 - 64
Bear	Steiff	15in (38.1cm)	1907 - 64
Bear (*)	Steiff	15in (38.1cm)	c1970 - 85
Bear (*)	Steiff	15in (38.1cm)	c1977 - 90
Bear	Steiff	16in (40.6cm)	1905 - 54
Bear	Steiff	16in (40.6cm)	1905 - 55
Bear (*)	Steiff	16in (40.6cm)	c1970 - 87
Bear (*)	Steiff	16in (40.6cm)	c1975 - 88
Bear	Steiff	17in (43.2cm)	1905 - 55
Bear	Steiff	17in (43.2cm)	1907 - 65
Bear	Steiff	17in (43.2cm)	1958 - 78
Bear	Steiff	17in (43.2cm)	1980 - 92
Bear (*)	Steiff	17in (43.2cm)	1980 - 39
Bear (*)	Steiff	17in (43.2cm)	1980 - 92
Bear	Steiff	18in (45.7cm)	1907 - 65
Bear (*)	Steiff	18in (45.7cm)	c1910 - 69
Bear (*)	Steiff	19in (48.3cm)	1905 - 56
Bear	Steiff	20in (50.8cm)	1905 - 56
Bear	Steiff	20in (50.8cm)	c1930 - 72
Bear	Steiff	20in (50.8cm)	1954 - 76
Bear	Steiff	22in (55.9cm)	c1930 - 72
Bear	Steiff	22in (55.9cm)	c1950 - 75
Bear	Steiff	24in (61.0cm)	c1905 - 57
Bear (*)	Steiff	24in (61.0cm)	1957 - 77
Bear (*)	Steiff	24in (61.0cm)	1978 - 90
Bear	Steiff	25in (63.5cm)	c1940 - 74
Bear	Steiff	26in (66.0cm)	1907 - 66
Bear	Steiff	28in (71.1cm)	c1930 - 73
Bear (*)	Steiff	33in (83.8cm)	c1970 - 86
Bear (*)	Strauss	14in (35.6cm)	1906 - 150
Bear	Unknown	3in (7.6cm)	c1915 - 162
Bear (*)	Unknown (Japan)	3in (7.6cm)	c1935 - 179
Bear	Unknown (Japan)	3in (7.6cm)	c1936 - 179
Bear (*)	Unknown (Japan)	4in (10.2cm)	c1970 - 195
Bear	Unknown (Japan)	5in (12.7cm)	c1920 - 164
Bear	Unknown (Japan)	5in (12.7cm)	c1920 - 164
Bear (*)	Unknown (Japan)	5in (12.7cm)	c1930 - 169
Bear	Unknown (Japan)	5in (12.7cm)	c1930 - 168
Bear (*)	Unknown	5in (12.7cm)	1930 - 168
Bear (*)	Unknown (Ger.)	5in (12.7cm)	c1945 - 187
Bear	Unknown (Ger.)	5in (12.7cm)	c1960 - 193
Bear (*)	Unknown (Japan)	6in (15.2cm)	c1945 - 188
Bear (*)	Unknown	7in (17.8cm)	c1914 - 160
Bear (*)	Unknown	7in (17.8cm)	c1914 - 160
Bear (*)	Unknown (Ger.)	7in (17.8cm)	c1914 - 160
Bear (*)	Unknown	7in (17.8cm)	1914 - 160
Bear (*)	Unknown (Japan)	7in (17.8cm)	c1930 - 170

Bear (*)	Unknown (Japan)	7in (17.8cm)	c1930 - 170
Bear (*)	Unknown (Ger.)	7in (17.8cm)	c1950 - 189
Bear	Unknown	8in (20.3cm)	c1910 - 155
Bear (*)	Unknown	8in (20.3cm)	c1930 - 170
Bear (*)	Unknown (Ger.)	8in (20.3cm)	c1950 - 189
Bear (*)	Unknown (Swiss)	8in (20.3cm)	c1950 - 190
Bear	Unknown (China)	8in (20.3cm)	c1980 - 197
Bear (*)	Unknown	9in (22.9cm)	c1930 - 171
Bear	Unknown (Ger.)	9in (22.9cm)	c1950 - 191
Bear (*)	Unknown	10in (25.4cm)	1908 - 154
Bear (*)	Unknown	10in (25.4cm)	1923 - 167
Bear	Unknown	10in (25.4cm)	c1930 -172
Bear (*)	Unknown	10in (25.4cm)	c1930 - 173
Bear	Unknown	10in (25.4cm)	c1940 - 181
Bear	Unknown	11in (27.9cm)	c1920 - 164
Bear (*)	Unknown (Korea)	11in (27.9cm)	1983 - 198
Bear	Unknown	12in (30.5cm)	c1903 - 151
Bear	Unknown	12in (30.5cm)	c1912 - 159
Bear	Unknown (Amer.)	12in (30.5cm)	c1930 - 159
Bear (*)	Unknown	12in (30.5cm)	c1930 - 174
Bear (*)	Unknown (Ger.)	12in (30.5cm)	1932 -179
Bear (*)	Unknown	12in (30.5cm)	1936 -180
Bear	Unknown	12in (30.5cm)	c1940 -182
Bear	Unknown (German)	13in (33.0cm)	c1950 - 82
Bear	Unknown	13in (33.0cm)	c1910 -155
Bear (*)	Unknown	13in (33.0cm)	c1915 -163
Bear (*)	Unknown	13in (33.0cm)	c1930 -174
Bear	Unknown	13in (33.0cm)	c1940 -183
Bear	Unknown (Ger.?)	14in (35.6cm)	c1907 -153
Bear	Unknown	14in (35.6cm)	c1910 -156
Bear (*)	Unknown	14in (35.6cm)	1930 -175
Bear	Unknown (Amer.)	14in (35.6cm)	c1940 -184
Bear (*)	Unknown	14in (35.6cm)	c1940 -184
Bear	Unknown (German)	14in (35.6cm)	c1950 -192
Bear	Unknown	14in (35.6cm)	c1960 -194
Bear	Unknown (Ger.)	15in (38.1cm)	c1908 -154
Bear	Unknown	15in (38.1cm)	c1910 -156
Bear	Unknown (Ger.)	15in (38.1cm)	c1925 -167
Bear	Unknown	15in (38.1cm)	c1930 -174
Bear (*)	Unknown	15in (38.1cm)	c1930 -174
Bear	Unknown (Amer.)	15in (38.1cm)	1940 -184
Bear	Unknown	15in (38.1cm)	c1940 -184
Bear (*)	Unknown	16in (40.6cm)	1910 -156
Bear (*)	Unknown	16in (40.6cm)	1926 -168
Bear	Unknown	16in (40.6cm)	c1930 -176
Bear (*)	Unknown	16in (40.6cm)	1931 -179
Bear (*)	Unknown (Japan)	16in (40.6cm)	c1940 -184
Bear	Unknown	17in (43.2cm)	c1907 -153
Bear (*)	Unknown	17in (43.2cm)	c1914 -160

Bear (*)	Unknown	17in (43.2cm)	1914 - 160
Bear	Unknown	17in (43.2cm)	c1915 -163
Bear (*)	Unknown	17in (43.2cm)	c1923 - 166
Bear	Unknown	17in (43.2cm)	c1930 - 176
Bear (*)	Unknown	18in (45.7cm)	c1890 - 152
Bear	Unknown	18in (45.7cm)	c1930 - 177
Bear	Unknown	18in (45.7cm)	c1930 - 177
Bear	Unknown (Amer.)	18in (45.7cm)	1936 - 180
Bear (*)	Unknown	18in (45.7cm)	1937 - 180
Bear	Unknown (Amer.)	18in (45.7cm)	c1940 - 184
Bear	Unknown (U.S.A.)	18in (45.7cm)	c1940 - 185
Bear (*)	Unknown (German)	19in (48.3cm)	c1925 - 167
Bear (*)	Unknown	19in (48.3cm)	c1930 - 177
Bear	Unknown (France)	19in (48.3cm)	c1939 - 181
Bear	Unknown	19in (48.3cm)	c1950 - 192
Bear (*)	Unknown (Ger.)	19in (48.3cm)	1979 - 196
Bear	Unknown (Ideal?)	20in (50.8cm)	c1910 - 157
Bear (*)	Unknown	20in (50.8cm)	1914 - 160
Bear (*)	Unknown	20in (50.8cm)	c1930 - 178
Bear (*)	Unknown (Taiwan)	20in (50.8cm)	1977 - 195
Bear (*)	Unknown	22in (55.9cm)	c1880 - 150
Bear	Unknown	22in (55.9cm)	1945 - 189
Bear	Unknown (Eng.)	23in (58.4cm)	c1910 - 157
Bear	Unknown	25in (63.5cm)	c1910 - 158
Bear	Unknown	25in (63.5cm)	c1940 - 184
Bear	Unknown (Eng.)	26in (66.0cm)	c1940 - 186
Bear	Unknown	32in (81.3cm)	c1920 - 164
Bear (*)	Wilkinson Mfg.	16in (40.6cm)	1981 -210
Bird	Steiff	1in (2.5cm)	c1955 - 95
Bird (*)	Steiff	2in (5.1cm)	c1950 - 94
Bird (*)	Steiff	2in (5.1cm)	c1950 - 94
Bird	Steiff	2in (5.1cm)	c1950 - 94
Bird (*)	Steiff	4in (10.2cm)	1958 - 95
Bird (*)	Steiff	4in (10.2cm)	c1977 - 96
Bird (*)	Steiff	6in (15.2cm)	1958 - 95
Boar (*)	Steiff	8in (20.3cm)	c1976 - 95
Camel	Steiff	6in (15.2cm)	1959 - 97
Camel	Unknown	12in (30.5cm)	c1880 -199
Carriage	Steiff	51in (127.0cm)	c1910 -97
Cat	Averill (German)	5in (12.7cm)	c1930 - 17
Cat (*)	Chad Valley	12in (30.5cm)	c1940 - 19
Cat	Steiff	3in (7.6cm)	c1900 - 98
Cat	Steiff	4in (10.2cm)	c1900 - 100
Cat	Steiff	4in (10.2cm)	c1950 - 99
Cat	Steiff	4in (10.2cm)	c1960 - 99
Cat	Steiff	4in (10.2cm)	c1978 - 102
Cat	Steiff	6in (15.2cm)	c1970 - 101
Cat	Steiff	7in (17.8cm)	c1960 - 101

Cat	Steiff	9in (22.9cm)	c1950 - 100
Cat	Steiff	10in (25.4cm)	c1978 - 102
Cat (*)	Steiff	3in (7.6cm)	1960 - 101
Cat (*)	Steiff	4in (10.2cm)	c1960 - 99
Cat	Unknown	10in (25.4cm)	c1930 - 200
Cat	Unknown	15in (38.1cm)	c1965 - 201
Cat (*)	Unknown (Ger.)	10in (25.4cm)	c1914 - 202
Chimp (*)	Schuco (?)	9in (22.9cm)	c1930 - 49
Chimp	Steiff	31in (78.7cm)	1957 - 103
Cock	Steiff	11in (27.9cm)	1960 - 103
Cow	Steiff	5in (12.7cm)	c1960 - 104
Cow (*)	Steiff	6in (15.2cm)	1960 - 105
Dinosaur	Steiff	13in (33.0cm)	c1955 - 104
Dog (*)	Averill	5in (12.7cm)	c1930 - 17
Dog	Steiff	3in (7.6cm)	c1950 - .06
Dog	Steiff	5in (12.7cm)	c1900 - 98
Dog	Steiff	17in (43.2cm)	c1960 - 107
Dog (*)	Steiff	3in (7.6cm)	1959 - 108
Dog (*)	Steiff	4in (10.2cm)	1960 - 111
Dog (*)	Steiff	4in (10.2cm)	1978 - 110
Dog (*)	Steiff	6in (15.2cm)	c1900 - 106
Dog (*)	Steiff	9in (22.9cm)	1907 - 61
Dog (*)	Steiff	9in (22.9cm)	1957 - 108
Dog (*)	Steiff	10in (25.4cm)	1959 - 109
Dog (*)	Steiff	12in (30.5cm)	1959 - 109
Dog (*)	Steiff	13in (33.0cm)	c1950 - 108
Dog (*)	Steiff	13in (33.0cm)	c1950 - 108
Dog (*)	Steiff	13in (33.0cm)	c1960 - 109
Dog	Unknown	13in (33.0cm)	c1945 - 203
Dog (*)	Unknown	9in (22.9cm)	c1910 - 204
Dog (*)	Unknown (Japan)	10in (25.4cm)	c1960 - 204
Dog (*)	Unknown	12in (30.5cm)	c1910 - 204
Doll (*)	Steiff	8in (20.3cm)	1978 - 110
Donkey (*)	Hermann	11in (27.9cm)	c1950 - 24
Donkey	Steiff	5in (12.7cm)	c1910 - 111
Donkey	Steiff	5in (12.7cm)	c1910 - 111
Duck (*)	Steiff	2in (5.8cm)	1950 - 94
Duck (*)	Steiff	3in (7.6cm)	c1950 - 94
Duck	Steiff	6in (15.2cm)	c1900 - 98
Duck	Steiff	6in (15.2cm)	1957 - 111
Duck	Steiff	6in (15.2cm)	1957 - 112
Elephant	Steiff	4in (10.2cm)	1958 112
Elephant	Steiff	4in (10.2cm)	c1977 - 113
Elephant	Steiff	7in (17.8cm)	c1977 - 113
Elephant	Steiff	7in (17.8cm)	c1977 - 113
Elephant	Steiff	8in (20.3cm)	c1977 - 114
Elephant	Steiff	9in (22.9cm)	1958 - 112
Elephant	Steiff	15in (38.1cm)	c1977 - 114
Fawn	Steiff	9in (22.9cm)	c1960 - 115

Frog	Steiff	3in (7.6cm)	c1940 -116
Giraf. (*)	Steiff	16in (40.6cm)	c1960 -117
Goat (*)	Steiff	6in (15.2cm)	c1960 -118
Hamster (*)	Steiff	4in (10.2cm)	1960 -118
Hedgehog	Steiff	5in (12.7cm)	1960 -119
Hen	Steiff	4in (10.2cm)	1959 -120
Hen	Steiff	9in (22.9cm)	1960 120
Horse (*)	Steiff	22in (55.9cm)	c1900 -120
Horse	Steiff	27in (68.6cm)	c1910 -120
Horse (*)	Unknown (Ger.)	7in (17.8cm)	c1890 -206
Horse (*)	Unknown (Ger.)	14in (35.6cm)	c1880 -204
Horse (*)	Unknown (Ger.)	16in (40.6cm)	c1890 -206
Horse (*)	Unknown	24in (61.0cm)	c1940 -207
Kangaroo	Steiff	11in (27.9cm)	c1960 -120
Koala (*)	R.D. France	15in (38.1cm)	c1930 - 41
Koala	Steiff	15in (38.1cm)	1950 -120
Koala	Uknown	16in (40.6cm)	c1935 -208
Koala	Unknown	17in (43.2cm)	c1935 -207
Lamb	Steiff	4in (10.2cm)	c1950 -106
Lamb (*)	Steiff	4in (10.2cm)	1978 -110
Lion (*)	Steiff	6in (15.2cm)	c1950 -122
Lion (Cub)	Steiff	8in (20.3cm)	1958 -122
Llama	Steiff	11in (27.9cm)	1957 -123
Monkey (*)	Schuco (?)	5in (12.7cm)	c1930 - 50
Monkey (*)	Steiff	10in (25.4cm)	1950 -126
Monkey	Steiff	11in (27.9cm)	c1930 -125
Monkey	Steiff	15in (38.1cm)	1977 -126
Monkey	Steiff	22in (55.9cm)	c1910 -124
Monkey	Unknown (USA?)	10in (25.4cm)	c1940 -208
Orang. (*)	Merry Thought	22in (55.9cm)	c1940 - 36
Owl (*)	Steiff	4in (10.2cm)	1960 -127
Owl (*)	Steiff	6in (15.2cm)	1960 -127
Owl (*)	Steiff	9in (22.9cm)	1960 -127
Owl (*)	Steiff	12in (30.5cm)	1960 -127
Panda (*)	Ideal	12in (30.5cm)	1945 - 32
Panda (*)	Ideal	18in (45.7cm)	1945 - 32
Panda	Steiff	6in (15.2cm)	c1950 -128
Parakeet	Steiff	4in (10.2cm)	c1977 - 96
Parrot (*)	Steiff	9in (22.9cm)	1976 -129
Pengn. (*)	Steiff	5in (12.7cm)	c1950 -116
Pidgeon	Steiff	3in (7.6cm)	c1950 - 94
Pidgeon	Steiff	8in (20.3cm)	c1980 -129
Pig	Mme. Alexander	11in (27.9cm)	c1940 - 37
Pig	Mme. Alexander	11in (27.9cm)	c1940 - 37
Pig	Mme. Alexander	11in (27.9cm)	c1940 - 37
Pig	Steiff	3in (7.6cm)	c1960 -130
Pig	Steiff	8in (20.3cm)	c1960 -130
Possum (*)	Unknown (Japan)	9in (22.9cm)	c1909 -208
Rabbit (*)	Mme. Alexander	14in (35.6cm)	c1930 - 38

Rabbit (*)	R.D. Co. (France)	12in (30.5cm)	c1900 - 42
Rabbit (*)	Steiff	3in (7.6cm)	1957 -139
Rabbit	Steiff	3in (7.6cm)	1959 -142
Rabbit	Steiff	6in (15.2cm)	c1930 -130
Rabbit	Steiff	6in (15.2cm)	1957 -140
Rabbit (*)	Steiff	6in (15.2cm)	1957 -139
Rabbit	Steiff	6in (15.2cm)	1958 -140
Rabbit	Steiff	7in (17.8cm)	c1950 -134
Rabbit (*)	Steiff	7in (17.8cm)	1957 -139
Rabbit (*)	Steiff	8in (20.3cm)	1959 -142
Rabbit (*)	Steiff	9in (22.9cm)	1948 -131
Rabbit (*)	Steiff	9in (22.9cm)	1948 -131
Rabbit	Steiff	9in (22.9cm)	c1948 -132
Rabbit (*)	Steiff	10in (25.4cm)	1957 -140
Rabbit (*)	Steiff	11in (27.9cm)	1948 -133
Rabbit (*)	Steiff	11in (27.9cm)	c1950 -134
Rabbit (*)	Steiff	12in (30.5cm)	1951 -138
Rabbit (*)	Steiff	13in (33.0cm)	c1950 -135
Rabbit	Steiff	13in (33.0cm)	1965 -143
Rabbit (*)	Steiff	14in (35.6cm)	c1950 -136
Rabbit (*)	Steiff	15in (38.1cm)	1977 - 90
Rabbit	Steiff	16in (40.6cm)	1977 -145
Rabbit (*)	Steiff	17in (43.2cm)	c1976 - 90
Rabbit	Steiff	18in (45.7cm)	1958 -141
Rabbit	Steiff	18in (45.7cm)	c1960 -143
Rabbit (*)	Steiff	18in (45.7cm)	c1970 -144
Rabbit (*)	Steiff	23in (58.4cm)	c1950 -137
Rabbit (*)	Steiff	23in (58.4cm)	c1970 -144
Rabbit (*)	Steiff	23in (58.4cm)	c1970 -144
Rabbit (*)	Unknown	9in (22.9cm)	c1936 -209
Rabbit (*)	Unknown (German)	13in (33.0cm)	c1907 -209
Rabbit (*)	Unknown (German)	15in (38.1cm)	c1907 -209
Ram	Unknown	12in (30.5cm)	c1880 -210
Ram (*)	Steiff	7in (17.8cm)	c1960 -146
Reindeer	Steiff	10in (25.4cm)	c1950 -147
Rooster	Steiff	4in (10.2cm)	1959 -147
Sheep (*)	Steiff	4in (10.2cm)	1978 -110
Squirrel	Steiff	8in (20.3cm)	1960 -119
Tiger Cub	Steiff	4in (10.2cm)	c1950 - 99
Tiger	Steiff	9in (22.9cm)	c1950 -148
Tiger	Steiff	12in (30.5cm)	c1970 -148
Turkey	Steiff	3in (7.6cm)	c1950 -149
Turkey	Steiff	5in (12.7cm)	c1958 -149
Turtle	Steiff	6in (15.2cm)	1957 -149
Turtle (*)	Steiff	12in (30.5cm)	c1977 -150
Walrus (*)	Steiff	5in (12.7cm)	c1950 -116
Wolf (*)	Gund	28in (71.1cm)	c1960 - 23

Related Items

Baby Rattle	Unknown (Eng.)	4in (10.2cm)	1910 - 220
Bank	Unknown	5in (12.7cm)	c1940 - 222
Bank	Unknown	7in (17.8cm)	c1910 - 222
Bank	Unknown	10in (25.4cm)	1907 - 220
Book	Bubbs-Merrill	11in (27.9cm)	1909 - 212
Book	Saalfield Pub.	15in (38.1cm)	1937 - 216
Book	Edw. Stern & Co.	11in (27.9cm)	1907 - 214
Book	Donahue & Co.	13in (33.0cm)	1907 - 213
Bookends	Unknown	7in (17.8cm)	c1930 - 224
Booklet	Steiff	4in (10.2cm)	1953 - 218
Booklet	Steiff	6in (15.2cm)	1958 - 218
Calendar	Unknown	8in (20.3cm)	1927 - 223
Campaign Flag	D & C, N.Y.	25in (63.5cm)	1912 - 212
Cigar Label	Schmidt & Co.	8in (20.3cm)	1903 - 216
Coat, Child's	Unknown	2 yr. old.	1907 - 220
Cookie Tin	Edward Sharp.	9in (22.9cm)	c1940 - 214
Crib Blanket	Esmond	36in (91.4cm)	c1920 - 214
Flatware	Unknown (Ger.)	4in (10.2cm)	c1930 - 224
Footstool	Steiff	15in (38.1cm)	c1977 - 218
Jewelry	Unknown	2in (5.1cm)	1927 - 220
Jewelry	Unknown	2in (5.1cm)	c1950 - 220
Milk Glass Plate	Unknown (Amer.)	7in (17.8cm)	1907 - 429
Muff	Unknown	12in (30.5cm)	c1930 - 225
Paper Doll	Ottmann Litho.	10in (25.4cm)	c1907 - 216
Salt & Pepper	Goebel	3in (7.6cm)	c1970 - 215
Salt & Pepper	Unknown	3in (7.6cm)	c1930 - 223
Sheet Music	Sherman Clay	12in (30.5cm)	1922 - 218
Silver Mug	Forbes Silver	3in (7.6cm)	c1915 - 215
Souvenir Spoon	Durgin Silver	6in (15.2cm)	c1907 - 213
Souvenir Spoon	Wm. Rogers Co.	6in (15.2cm)	c1970 - 213
Tape Measure	Unknown (Japan)	3in (7.6cm)	c1930 - 224
Tea Set	Unknown (Ger.)		1907 - 219
Tea Set	Unknown (Japan)		c1930 - 223
T.R. Doll	Nisbet	8in (20.3cm)	1983 - 217
T.R. Doll	Schoenhut	8in (20.3cm)	1908 - 217
T.R. Photo	Unknown	10in (25.4cm)	1935 - 225
Umbrella	Stella Olsen	Adult size	1978 - 219
Valentine	Raphael Tuck	12in (30.5cm)	c1909 - 216

Notes

Notes

About The Author

Helen Sieverling was born in the state of Kansas. It was there she grew up and received her education. She was one of three little girls born into the home of a young minister and his wife. Her childhood memories are happy ones.

Teddy bears and dolls were very much a part of her early life. The Teddy bear she remembers best was a large brown bear given to "my sister and me to share. We shared and loved him for many years and he seems to be the one I remember most." This teddy bear was only one of many who lived in the parsonage with them as Christmas usually brought a teddy bear.

Her husband, Glenn, has worked many hours at her side sharing the work in this book as well as photographing many of the items priced therein.

She has collected dolls for 20 years and has been a serious teddy bear collector for the last 10 years. She helped start the first teddy bear club in southern California, called the Teddy Bear Boosters, and was an officer for the first few years. She and her husband, Glenn, have shared their bears with many southern California clubs, some of them not related to the doll world —but teddy bears bring interest and happiness to any group.

Helen and Glenn Sieverling sincerely hope this book will be helpful to you as you pursue your hobby and quest for Teddy and his friends.

Update on Teddy Bear and friends ™ Price Guide

A feature article is provided in each issue of *Teddy Bear and friends ™* magazine as an opportunity to update prices and to add new entries from now to the release of the next edition of this price guide.

Helen Sieverling

Subscribe Now...
The Teddy Bear and friends™ Magazine

Issued quarterly The Teddy Bear and friends ™ Magazine 1 year **$9.95** with beautiful color photography. Articles aimed at serious collectors and makers of Teddy Bears.